VOCAL MEDICINE
Transformation through Sound

VOCAL MEDICINE
Transformation through Sound

An Introduction to Mantras, Chanting and Kirtan

Kathleen Karlsen

Copyright ©2019 Kathleen Karlsen, Living Arts Enterprises, LLC

Illustrations by Rose Karlsen
Cover artwork by Kathleen Karlsen
Cover design by Andrew Karlsen
Music by Kathleen Karlsen (unless noted as traditional)

kathleenkarlsen.com

All rights reserved. No part of this material may be reproduced by any means, including mechanical, photographic, electronic or verbal recording or otherwise copied for public or private use without prior written permission of the author.

The information, insights and recommendations contained in this book are based on the research, opinions and experiences of the author. The information provided is for educational purposes. This book is not intended to diagnose, cure or prevent disease. Please see appropriate medical practitioners for health issues.

Anahata Publications

ISBN: 978-0-9833583-1-2
Library of Congress Control Number 2019902369
Printed in the United States of America

Gratitude

With deepest gratitude
for the spiritual truth in all traditions,
for my personal teachers,
for my wonderful friends,
and for my beautiful family.

TABLE OF CONTENTS

Part I: Introduction to Mantras
1: Reforge Your Heart with Mantras..3
2: Science of Mantras..9
3: Building Blocks of Sound..15
4: Formulas for Freedom..21
5: Sounds of the Cosmos..33

Part II: Transformation and the Chakras
6: Wheels of Fire: The Seven Chakras..43
7: Establishing Safety: Base Chakra..49
8: Healing Relationships: Sacral Chakra.......................................55
9: Honoring Intuition: Solar Plexus Chakra..................................59
10: Giving Devotion: Heart Chakra..63
11: Mastering Power: Throat Chakra..67
12: Holding a Vision: Third Eye Chakra..75
13: Finding Unity: Crown Chakra..83

Part III: Enhancing the Power of Mantras
14: Synergy of the Body and Soul..91
15: Sound, Color and Kirtan...97
16: Mantras and Yantras..105

Part IV: Songs of Transformation
17: Finding Bliss through Kirtan..119
18: Goddess Chants...129
19: Chants for Peace...141
20: Chants of Divine Love..149
21: Chants of Victory..157

Bibliography..167
Index..169
Resources..172

PART I
Introduction to Mantras

Chapter 1
Reforge Your Heart with Mantras

I know what it's like to have pain in your heart that keeps you awake at night. That kind of feeling is shockingly physical and makes it hard to breathe or move or think. You don't know how or when your suffering will end and whether hope and joy will ever return.

Everyone experiences heartbreak of some kind. I suppose we are each affected to different degrees by different types of experiences. The depth of the anguish seems to be related to the significance of the event in your life and the things that matter to you the most.

The situation may be an illness, a death, an accident, financial loss, physical or emotional trauma, or the breakdown of a partnership. A few years ago I was in the most deeply unhappy period of my life. At the same time, I was passionately pursuing a new way to heal myself—I was chanting.

Forging a New Heart

No matter how desolate I was feeling during that time, every morning I got up and drove my car to an isolated spot (to avoid disturbing my family), turned on my music and began to chant. This was a huge effort on many levels. For one thing, I had to breathe to chant or sing. Sometimes I couldn't breathe without feeling the pain.

Occasionally I ended up sobbing for an hour or more instead of chanting. Sometimes I couldn't even make a sound, so I poured out my heart in my journal. Then I would try to chant again. Whatever I was feeling, I had to move through it in order to chant.

As the weeks and months went by, chanting established a new rhythm in my life. Day after day, I chanted in those early mornings in my car, parked at the foot of one hiking trail or another near my home in Bozeman, Montana. I chanted each day as the darkness faded and the sun rose over the mountains. Winter turned into spring, then summer and fall. I was healing. My life was shifting and expanding in ways I had never imagined. A new heart had been forged and a new life had begun.

At first I wasn't interested in teaching others to chant. All I really wanted to do was heal myself. However, in the process of chanting I discovered something unexpected: a broken heart that has healed is even stronger than one that has never been touched by trauma or loss or disappointment. I am not saying that a heart that is healed never again feels the sorrow from past traumas or the pain of present realities. It is actually quite the opposite.

A heart that is healed feels both the pain and the joy of life more keenly than ever before. Perhaps that is the price to be paid for healing enough that you choose again to live with an open heart. In the process of healing, the capacity of the heart seems to be increased. Connecting to others and sharing with others seems to be a natural outcome of that expansion.

Healing through Spiritual Fire

I imagine that the healing of the heart through chanting is similar to the reforging of the shards of Narsil in the *Lord of the Rings* trilogy. Narsil was the sword that Isildur used to cut the One Ring from Sauron's hand. The sword was shattered into many pieces, and later was reforged with physical fire into Andúril, the sword of Aragorn, the new king. In my experience, a heart can be reforged by spiritual fire.

Chanting is one of the most effective ways to bring spiritual fire into the heart itself and into the heart chakra, the energy center associated with your physical heart. Spiritual fire purifies, heals and creates new connections to stitch the heart back together.

This may also be similar to what has been revealed through neuroscience: an injured brain creates new connections and pathways to restore full functioning. This process actually increases the plasticity of the brain. The connections in the heart are like the new neurons in the brain, or like the seams of welded steel that mend a sword, but they are flexible and soften the heart rather than making it more rigid.

The process of healing gives you the confidence to be vulnerable again. You still remember the grief, but you have a way to endure and to restore your faith in life and love and God. When you know that you can survive and you can heal, that confidence makes you willing to risk that pain again and to continue to grow. You fear the challenges of life less and recognize the blessings more.

I have had the opportunity to meet many others with similar experiences of healing themselves and their hearts with chanting. The name of God on your lips and the vibration of His chants in your heart can create a miracle. The process of healing through mantras and chanting is what I am now calling vocal medicine.

Mantras and the Yoga of Sound

The power of the voice to transform our hearts, minds and spirits may be one of the reasons why devotional singing exists in virtually all cultures and traditions. The Eastern form of devotional singing is known as Mantra Yoga.

Mantra is derived from two Sanskrit words. There are many interpretations of the word mantra. Most sources say that "man" is from "manas" or mind. Some sources say that "tra" is from "trai," meaning to protect or free from. So a mantra would protect you from distractions and free you from the prison of your mind.

Many experts say that "mantra" means "a sacred text or message." Still other sources say that "tra" means "a vehicle or instrument to concentrate the mind." All of these interpretations indicate that mantras are types of worded formulas or sound tools with distinct impacts on emotional, mental and spiritual states.

Mantra Yoga is a central practice of Bhakti Yoga, a form of yoga that emphasizes devotion. This is the path of the heart. Bhakti Yoga can include any one of many different physical yoga practices or none at all. Bhakti Yoga is often focused on a personal aspect of God such as the Divine Mother or a particular deity.

The yoga of sound is known as Naad or Nada Yoga. This includes both chanting and instrumental music. "Naad" is the Sanskrit word for "sound or tone." The entire universe consists of sound or vibration. Naad can be interpreted as the flow of sound. "Yoga" means "to unite, connect or integrate." Yoga is the union of polarities or differentiated aspects of life: mind and body; spirit and matter; masculine and feminine. Naad Yoga is the use of sound to unite polarities on one or more levels.

Discovering Chanting and Kirtan

Chanting utilizes many concrete elements—sound, voice, rhythm and melody—to express love and to draw down the energy of life and spirit. I was first exposed to Eastern chanting in my early twenties while still in college. At the time, I was exploring many different paths and alternative healing practices. I attended a number of conferences on these topics. One evening at a self-improvement seminar, we spent a brief period chanting a single mantra. This was my first experience with kirtan. Kirtan is chanting in a group, often with a leader in a call and response format. I immediately connected with the practice.

After returning home, I spent my early mornings chanting alone on my porch. I gathered scraps of wood from local construction sites and built a small fire in a hibachi grill so that I could focus on the flames while I chanted. I knew no one else who chanted. I only knew one mantra: Om Namah Shivaya, a chant honoring Shiva, one of the three gods of the Hindu trinity. I had no idea that there were thousands of ancient chants and millions of people chanting across the globe.

When I went back to college, I moved into a student apartment and couldn't find a place to chant. As a result, I continued with other spiritual practices, including a form of spoken prayers known as decrees.[1] Decrees involve many of the same elements as mantras. They consist of repeated verses that are said aloud on a particular pitch. The pitch usually rises and the speed of the decree often increases as the repetitions continue. Like chants, spoken decrees can be given alone or in a group.

In my twenties I spent over a decade almost exclusively in the spiritual practice of decrees, often five hours or more a day. I enjoyed the practice and felt that it was highly beneficial. I still recite a set of decrees each morning before I begin chanting. Like mantras, decrees are structured for different purposes: protection, forgiveness, healing, prosperity and so forth.

Before I had children, I also was a member of a recording choir for a spiritual organization. That was an incredible experience. We created several CDs of music, sometimes spending half the night recording. I loved devotional singing more than any other form of prayer or worship, though it always seemed like a side dish rather than the main course. I was thrilled when I discovered through Bhakti yoga that chanting could be a central spiritual practice in and of itself.

My spiritual life went on hold for a couple decades in adulthood while I raised five kids and ran a multimedia business with my husband Andrew. Those years went by in a blur of diapers and meals and school events and running a large household and working long hours to pay the bills.

Learning to Lead Kirtan

About four years ago I rediscovered chanting and kirtan. I fell totally in love with the combination of singing sacred music and the feeling of community that is unique to the experience of kirtan. I began chanting an hour or two a day on my own and was attending kirtan twice a week with a small local group. When the group dispersed, I continued chanting alone for about six months. Chanting alone is fantastic, but I deeply missed the sense of community and connection with others that comes with kirtan. Finally I decided that I would learn to play the harmonium (a musical instrument often central to kirtan) and lead chants myself. I had never sung in public and I was quite terrified. However, my desire to recreate the magical experience of kirtan drove me to overcome my fear.

I took some beginning harmonium lessons with Jake Fleming, a multi-talented local musician, and started inviting one or two friends over on Sunday afternoons to chant in my living room. After a couple of months, Jake gave me the opportunity to lead some chants at a few of his kirtans. At that point I came across the website of Mike Cohen, founder of the Kirtan Leadership Institute in Boulder, Colorado. Attending his training program in kirtan leadership was a turning point. Coming back home to Bozeman, I rented space in yoga studios and started holding my own kirtans.

Things expanded rapidly from there: other musicians joined me to form a kirtan band, and a chanting community began to grow. I also started sharing my experiences and studies of mantras and chanting in workshops. Eventually I commissioned my daughter Rose, an illustrator, to create illustrations for educational materials and kirtan lyric sheets. This reignited my own love of sacred art and symbolism. All of this created wonderful avenues for serving others.

One of my greatest joys is to use the principles of chanting and mantras to create music and experiences that are relatable and understandable in today's world. I love both the ancient traditions and the modern science behind the effectiveness of this practice. I hope that my research and my personal experiences will inspire you to experiment for yourself with vocal medicine and transformation through sound.

Chapter 2
Science of Mantras

The repetition of a mantra is closely aligned with breathing practices. This does not even have to be a conscious effort. The rhythmic nature of a repeated mantra naturally creates a cyclical pattern of breathing. When people are singing or chanting together, studies have shown that their heart rates and breathing tend to synchronize.[2] This helps to create a sense of connection and community on multiple levels. In addition, many spiritual traditions view the breath as the bridge between the inner world and the outer world.

Controlling the breath or expanding the breath can change our perception of reality. Observing and adjusting the breath joins our minds and spirits to our bodies. The core of Mantra Yoga as well as other yoga practices is a direct experience of God. This is somatic spirituality or embodied spirituality versus an intellectual study or understanding of God.

Mantras as Energy Conductors

My personal experience of mantras is a very physical sensation of connecting with a source of energy. This creates a buzzing feeling like a vibrational humming throughout my entire body. Sometimes this is accompanied by a sensation of burning in my heart or the sensation of energy filling my chest. It is a euphoria a bit like a runner's high, only more pervasive. Sort of like being intoxicated in every cell.

This may happen quickly or slowly. I find the sensation builds the most when I am chanting the same mantra continuously for a period of time rather than moving from mantra to mantra. However, when and if this happens and how long it takes varies widely.

Sometimes it only takes ten minutes. Sometimes the feeling is completely elusive even in the course of an hour or two of chanting. Other times the energy flow starts without any chanting at all when I am merely thinking about chanting.

The sense of buzzing energy can build to the point where I am sure that I must be physically shaking, yet if I open my eyes and look at my arms and legs, they are motionless. Another way to explain this would be feeling like I have been connected to a powerful energy source. I feel the current flowing although there are no visible signs that anything has changed.

Mantras and Altered States of Consciousness

In addition to these physical sensations, repeated mantras can induce altered states of consciousness. Normal consciousness is defined in scientific circles as the state in which we are monitoring our environments and choosing how to respond. In an altered state of consciousness, our ability to monitor and control our responses is distorted.[3] We may become selectively aware of our environments or completely unaware of our surroundings.

Repeating a mantra also helps to calm an area of the brain known as the default mode network.[4] Calming or deactivating this area of the brain can help to relieve depression, anxiety, and even suicidal tendencies. In these fundamental ways, mantras can be used to gain freedom from a limited state of mind.

There is also scientific evidence that mantras revitalize the physical body. The relaxation response (lowered heart rate, lower blood pressure, slower breathing rate) triggered by various forms of meditation and spiritual practices including mantra repetition has been well-documented by Herbert Benson, professor of medicine at Harvard Medical School.[5] Benson recommends the use of a mental device (such as word, phrase or repeated activity) to keep the mind focused. The goal is to activate the parasympathetic nervous system for relaxation.

Mantras, Meridians and the Brain

Furthermore, mantras and chanting stimulate the channels of energy in the body known as meridians. There are eighty-four meridians that end in the mouth. There are two meridians each for the thirty-two adult teeth in the hard palate and twenty additional meridians in the soft palate in the roof of the mouth.

Placement of the tongue in various positions to form words during speaking or chanting connects these meridians to the brain, increasing the energy flow to the pituitary, thalamus, hypothalamus and pineal glands. Each of these glands are important parts of the endocrine system. Moreover, they are purported in metaphysical and occult literature to have significant roles in the development of spiritual faculties.

The pituitary gland produces hormones that help to regulate the functions of other endocrine glands. The pituitary gland rests in a bony hollow in the brain directly behind and a little below the bridge of the nose. The pituitary is often called the master gland because of its control of the thyroid and adrenals as well as the ovaries and testicles.

The thalamus gland relays sensory information in the form of hormones from receptors in various parts of the body to the cerebral cortex. The hypothalamus affects temperature regulation, food intake, water intake, sleep and waking patterns, emotions and memory.

The pineal gland is known to produce melatonin, which helps to regulate sleep patterns. Scientifically speaking, the other functions of the pineal gland are not fully understood. From a mystical standpoint, entire books have been written about the pineal gland, which is said to be intimately connected to the third eye or Ajna chakra, an energy center in the forehead between the eyes.

The pineal gland is reputed to be the source of psychic vision or the "eye of God." The pineal gland is discussed extensively in Manly P. Hall's classic book *Man: The Grand Symbol of the Mysteries*. This gland "is regarded as a link between the objective and subjective states of consciousness; or, in exoteric terminology, the visible and invisible worlds of nature."[6]

The importance of the pineal gland in the development of higher consciousness is emphasized in many traditions. Some view the pineal gland as a receptor for spiritual vibrations, sort of a radio station between the physical and the spiritual worlds. René Descartes, the French scientist and philosopher, believed that the pineal gland was the "seat of the human soul."[7]

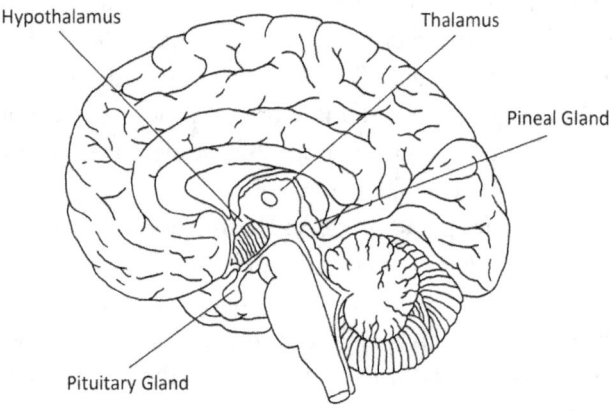

The Sanskrit Effect

The sounds that stimulate these spiritual centers in the brain are present in virtually every language. However, they are particularly prominent in Sanskrit, the most common language used in Eastern chanting and mantras. The positive impact on the brain for those learning mantras or reciting Sanskrit sacred texts is being referred to as the "Sanskrit effect."

James Hartzell, Ph.D., a neuroscientist researching the topic, has looked at the physical changes in the brain that happen during the memorization and recitation of Sanskrit texts. He discovered that Sanskrit pandits have over ten percent more grey matter across both cerebral hemispheres, a measurement consistent with higher cognitive functioning.

The right hippocampus, connected to long-term and short-term memory, is also sensitive to auditory and visual patterns. The hippocampus in the brains of Hartzell's subjects was shown to have more grey matter across nearly seventy-five percent of its structure.[8]

All languages have their own identity and characteristics. The emphasis on certain sounds creates a unique overall impact that can be recognized historically and energetically. Thus, French is considered to be a language of diplomacy and Italian has been viewed as the language of love. German has a grounding aspect and Spanish is a highly relational language. Some consider English to be a language descended from angelic tongues. Other liturgical languages like Latin, Hebrew, Greek and Gurmukhi have their own mystical and spiritual qualities.

Science is demonstrating that the ancient practice of mantras has concrete benefits. In this way, the recitation of mantras is both a spiritual practice and a practical art.

CHAPTER 3
Building Blocks of Sound

The understanding of chanting and the power of sound starts with the building blocks of music. I love to experiment with various tones and syllables when I am practicing privately. There is a purity and simplicity about producing tones with single syllables that appeals to me. This can be as simple as singing a scale.

Scales, Sargam and Solfeggio

Solemnization or solfeggio is the practice of using syllables to teach pitch and sight reading through recognition of the different steps of the scale. This practice originated in ancient India with a system known as sargam: SA, RE, GA, MA, PA, DHA, NI, SA.

A few thousand years later, a Benedictine monk named Guido d'Arezzo who was familiar with the Indian system noted that most of the Gregorian chants popular at that time could easily be learned by singers if they could see the tone progression up and down the scale. In this way, they could associate visual symbols with particular syllables and sounds.

Guido assigned specific syllables to each of the notes of the scale: Do, Re, Mi, Fa, Sol, La, Ti, Do. These syllables came from Ut Quent Laxis, a well-known hymn of the Middle Ages that was chanted for vespers. Each succeeding line of the song started one note higher that the previous one. Guido used the first two letters of the opening words from each line to create a western form of solemnization.

Vocal teachers have understood and taught this tonal progression in a variety of ways. A number of them have recognized that there is also an energy shift on a metaphysical level as you move through the notes of the scale. My experience has been that each note can be viewed as a shift in energy from unmanifest potential to unification. In other words, the sound and energy are more diffuse and grounded at the lower tones and concentrated like a laser beam as you move through the tones that are produced higher in the body, often referred to as head tones. From this standpoint, the following can be viewed as a general progression and shift of energy:

DO	Unmanifest Potential
RE	Felt Potential
MI	Gathering Energy
FA	Devotional Energy
SOL	Fearlessness
LA	Intuition
TI	Merging
DO	Unification

The Science of Vowels and Consonants

To break this down even further, the impact of vowels and consonants on the body and the mind is a science in and of itself. There appears to be a coded formula in many sacred languages that directly stimulates various systems and organs in the body. There are also mudras (hand positions) and body movements that correspond to each note of the scale.

At a fundamental level, vowels are feminine energy: consonants are masculine energy. Vowels are generic and formless. Consonants set parameters around the feminine energy to create form from formlessness. In other words, consonants create a container. The vowels can also be correlated with the five elements system utilized in feng shui and acupuncture as outlined below:

> **A (aye):** spiritual opening, passion, anger, wood element, liver and gallbladder
>
> **E (ee):** absolute discernment, joy, disappointment, fire element, heart and small intestines
>
> **I (eye):** totality of energy, concentration, will, brooding, earth element, spleen and pancreas
>
> **O (oh):** mental or intellectual activity, confidence, fear, water element, kidneys and bladder
>
> **U (ew):** potentiality, physicality, compassion, grief, metal element, lungs and large intestines

Every sound literally vibrates the cells, bones, organs, and fluids in the body. The sonic power of vowels is recognized in many languages and systems. In the eastern tradition, Sanskrit vowels correspond with various bodily systems:

> **AH (A):** assists with the health and strength of the lungs, energizes the mind
>
> **EE (E):** positive effect on the throat and the brain, alleviates depression
>
> **AI (I):** supports the health of the kidneys and urinary tract
>
> **OW (O):** strengthens the functioning of the reproductive system
>
> **UH (U):** supports a healthy heart and pumping of the blood throughout the body

The power of the vowels can be harnessed by controlling and directing them with the energy of the masculine consonants. A few examples of the role of consonants in words include:

> **L:** focuses energy in a chosen direction
> **M:** appreciation, continues spiritual action
> **N:** power, closing, very strong stopping point
> **S:** all directions, gathering (also SH, V, Z)
> **T:** explosion of energy (also D and B)
> **Y:** desire, agreement

It is interesting to note that the consonant "n" is used in many languages to indicate disagreement or an attempt to stop someone else: No! (English), Nee! (Afrikans), Niet! (Russian), Nein! (German), Nahi! (Hindi), Non! (French), Nei! (Norwegian). And the consonant "y" is often used to indicate union or an understanding: Yes. Yah. Yay. Yoga. Ye.

Seed Syllables and the Chakras

There are also fundamental sounds known as seed syllables for each of the chakras or energy centers in the body. (See Part II: Transformation and the Chakras, pp. 41-87.) The seed syllables are sounds that strengthen the positive aspects of each chakra respectively. Some systems use variations of these sounds or alternate sounds, especially for the crown chakra. The following are generally accepted as the seed syllables for the indicated chakras:

> **LAM:** base or root chakra
> **VAM:** sacral chakra
> **RAM:** solar plexus chakra
> **YAM:** heart chakra
> **HAM:** throat chakra
> **OM:** third eye chakra
> **AH*:** crown chakra
> (*sometimes ANG or AUM)

These building blocks have been used to create mantras and chants aimed at enhancing positive qualities within ourselves or ameliorating areas of weakness or challenge. Some of the effects can be documented scientifically. Others are based on long-standing traditions in various cultures. And some aspects of this practice are highly individual and experiential.

Chakra Mantras: Seed Syllables

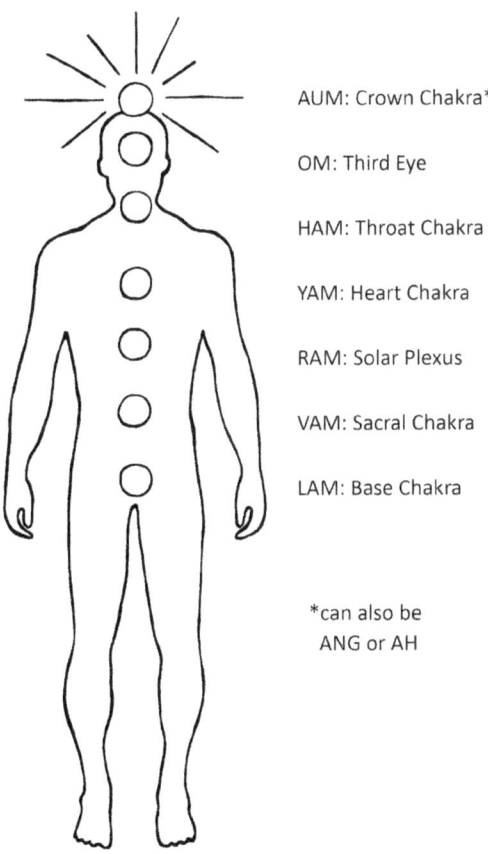

AUM: Crown Chakra*

OM: Third Eye

HAM: Throat Chakra

YAM: Heart Chakra

RAM: Solar Plexus

VAM: Sacral Chakra

LAM: Base Chakra

*can also be ANG or AH

Chants and Songs as Prayer

In addition, singing a melody rather than speaking a prayer integrates the emotional body in the practice of creating sound.

According to many religious historians, prayers were always sung in traditional practices and rituals including the Latin Mass in Catholicism, Jewish services of all types, and Hindu and Buddhist festivals, as well as indigenous and tribal rituals.

St. Augustine is said to have claimed, "He who sings prays twice." To engage the heart and the emotions in song may be twice as powerful as a spoken prayer. Jewish mystics believe that songs reach the realm of the angels and the throne of God.

CHAPTER 4
Formulas for Freedom

For thousands of years the rishis of India (Hindu sages) experimented with the effects of chanting. Mantras focused on the names of the gods and goddesses in the Hindu pantheon appear to be coded compilations of sound designed to create elevated states and to stimulate health and longevity. Mantras may be keys to connecting with and embodying the aspect of God's consciousness exemplified by a particular deity.

Specific Sounds and Human Wellness

When vowels and consonants are put together in words and phrases and mantras, formulas can be created with distinct impacts on emotional, mental and physical states. For example, the sound "uhm" or "ahm" is purported to energize and purify the blood. The "uh" is said to help to cleanse the body of impurities and the "m" seals the body from incoming negative energies.

Likewise, the sound "aha" is stimulating for the hormonal system. This exclamation is often used in English when a sudden solution or insight is gained (aha!). The Sanskrit translation means something very similar: "indeed, it is true, certainly, surely, it is granted."

When this sound is extended (a ha ha ha ha ha ha), the effect is similar to laughter therapy, which has been proven to relieve stress and depression. Indeed, laughing with friends is a powerful group bonding experience. We are thirty times more likely to laugh in a group context than when alone.

The Sanskrit word "namaha" combines the "aha" sound with two controlling consonants (n and m) and means "it is not about me; I submit to a higher power of control in my life." This word is utilized in many Eastern chants:

Om Namaha Sri—represents the process of letting go and giving of oneself
Om Namaha Shivaya—focuses on removing all that is not the divine within
Om Gam Ganapatiyei Namaha—removes obstacles and opens the door to success
Om Sri Kali Durgaya Namaha—provides protection and removes negativity within and without
Om Sri Ramaya Namaha—begets pure divine consciousness and truth

Another example is the syllable "la." Pronouncing this syllable involves the tongue and upper frontal part of the palate. This creates a conduction of energy to the brain. "La" is also a common syllable used for vocal exercises for singers.

In Sanskrit, "la" means "the act of giving or taking," as in an exchange. In the Hindu tradition, Lakshmi is the goddess of wealth, fortune, health and prosperity. Prosperity is the process of giving or exchanging a service or product. Here is an example of a chant to Lakshmi:

Om Shrim Maha Lakshmi Namaha—this combines om (the sound of universal creation) with shrim (the Sanskrit bija or seed syllable incorporated in the name Lakshmi) and maha (which simply meaning great) with namaha, meaning honor.

Another powerful healing mantra is the *Siri Gaitri Mantra*, sung in Gurmukhi, the liturgical language of the Sikh tradition.

This mantra taps into the energies of the sun, moon, earth and the Infinite Spirit to bring deep healing. It can be chanted to heal the self or to send healing energy to anyone you wish:

Ra Ma Da Sa, Sa Say So Hung—the meaning of this chant is ra (sun), ma (moon), da (earth), sa (impersonal infinity), say (totality), so (personal sense of merger and identity) and hung (the infinite, vibrating and real).

Chanting in Nature

The mastery of sound can also connect you to your environment. There are many indigenous traditions of singing to the wind, the rain and the earth. You can begin to work with natural elements and the weather. Personally I believe that all of life has some level of consciousness and sentience. This is a realm that I would like to explore further.

I had a remarkable experience a few years ago chanting in nature. Most people do not realize that there are megaliths here in Montana. Megaliths are large stones structures of various types akin to the more famous Stonehenge in Britain. A number of these megaliths are located about a ninety minute drive from my home in Bozeman.

My husband Andrew and I took a day-long tour of some of the megaliths with Julie Ryder, an avid researcher and expert on the topic (see Resources, p. 172). When our group had finished a fascinating day exploring the megaliths with Julie, I was standing near a unique structure called the Pink Vault.

The Pink Vault consists of two large pink granite boulders surrounded by a wall of black granite boulders. I found the structure to be particularly fascinating and attractive. Julie saw me from across a little valley and called over to me to chant.

I started chanting one of my favorite chants to Lalita, a Hindu goddess. My husband knew the song and began chanting with me. After a few minutes we rejoined the group.

Julie had filmed us chanting and thought she had turned off the camera. The next morning she discovered that the camera had actually been on for a few minutes after we had been chanting near the Pink Vault. She had captured an image of a waterfall of pink light cascading down in that spot.

I don't know if waterfall was related to me personally as much as to the chanting itself. In other words, for me this experience was a sign that the chanting was having an energetic impact in unseen dimensions. I find the memory of that pink waterfall to be comforting on days when I may not feel that my chants are making a difference for me or in the world at large. I have no real explanation for the pink waterfall, but something certainly seemed to be happening.

I am fortunate to be surrounded by beautiful creeks and rivers, vast mountains and splendid pine forests. Going forward, I would like to spend more time chanting among the rocks and trees.

Ayurvedic Healing Chants

There are specific chants in the Indian Ayurvedic system for all aspects of the subtle energy body that is surrounding and interpenetrating the physical body. The holistic science of Ayurvedic healing was developed in India over 3,000 years ago. According to Ayurvedic teachings, the subtle energy body can be harmonized to the physical body to create a flow of energy that assists and supports physical health. This energy body is known as the Mantra Purusha or the body of sound.

The Mantra Purusha correlates all of the vowels, consonants, semi-vowels and sibilants in the Sanskrit language to regions of the body. There are sixteen vowels, twenty-five consonants and nine semi-vowels and sibilants. Many of the vowels and corresponding syllables have both long and short vowel forms. The sounds and mantras correspond to zones known as the marmas that are similar to but larger than acupuncture points.

A great introductory handbook for this topic is *Mantra Yoga and Primal Sound* by Dr. David Frawley (Pandit Vamadeva Shasti). Dr. Frawley includes an appendix with mantras for each area of the body. Each mantra follows a pattern: the word "om" followed by the seed syllable for a specific part of the body, followed by the word "namah" and completed by the name of the bodily location.

For example, a possible mantra for the head is "Om Am Namah Sirasi," which translates something like: "O Universe, I give reverence to my head!" Likewise, the mantra "Om Im Namah Vama Netre" means "O Universe, I give reverence to my left eye!" The following are a few examples of mantras for the head region.

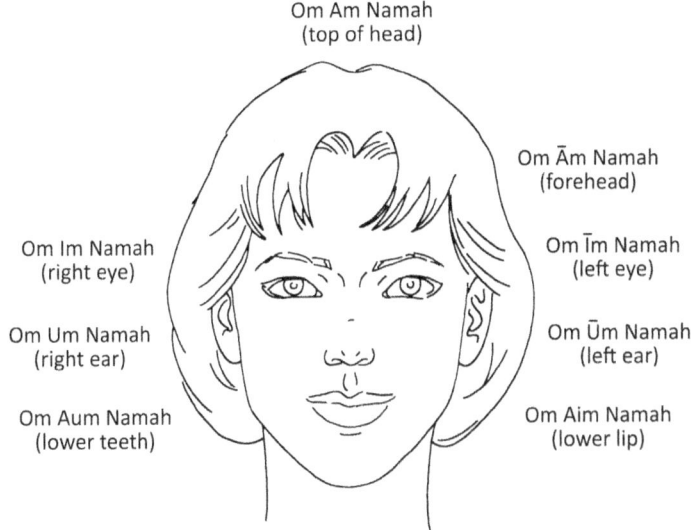

Body Intelligence

I find it fascinating that healing the body through giving homage and praise to the body itself is a principle that seems to be universal. This principle has been rediscovered in modern times by practitioners of positive thinking and New Thought Christianity. Myrtle and Charles Fillmore, founders of the Unity School of Christianity, both healed themselves of tuberculosis using this approach. Myrtle Fillmore relates her experience:

> Life is simply a form of energy and has to be guided and directed in man's body by his

> intelligence. How do we communicate with intelligence? By thinking and talking, of course....
>
> I told the life in my liver that I was not torpid or inert, but full of vigor and energy. I told the life in my stomach that it was not weak or inefficient, but energetic, strong and intelligent....I told my limbs that they were active and strong.
>
> I went to all of the life centers in my body and spoke words of Truth to them—words of strength and power....I did not become discouraged at their being slow to wake up, but kept right on, both silently and aloud, declaring the words of Truth, until the organs responded.[10]

Myrtle Fillmore's health began to improve immediately, she was completely free of tuberculosis in two years, and she went on to live another forty years founding and running a church and spiritual organization.

Chanting and Healing Affirmations

When healing affirmations and positive self-talk are set to music, they can be chanted for potentially even more effective results. By correlating the specific symbolic meaning of an aspect of the human body with the lyrics in the chants or songs that are chosen, you can be conscious of the benefits you seek to gain. I have created my own chants with affirmations in English related to eyesight and vision, thyroid health, general vitality and to help to heal a shoulder injury from a fall I had while hiking.

The meanings associated with different parts of the body are often revealed in our common idioms and colloquial expressions.

This correspondence between language and body meaning allows you to chant or sing with particular healing outcomes in mind.

I also like to use images of human anatomy for visualizations when chanting privately. I am thrilled by the capacity and the beauty of the human body. I love stories about extreme athletes and people with amazing physical abilities of all kinds.

As a child, I had planned to go into the medical field. However, as I observed life around me during my teenage years, the maladies of the mind and soul seemed much deeper than those of the body. I began to feel that the mind and spirit should be addressed first or at least simultaneously with the body.

This led me to study of the work of Louise Hay and other pioneers in the field of the mind-body connection. For decades there have been forerunners in metaphysics and psychology insisting that we recognize the importance of attitudes, emotions and beliefs in health and wellness. These include Dr. John Sarno, Steven Ray Ozanich, Deb Shapiro, Joe Dispenza, Inna Segal, Bernie Siegel and more. Some of these experts have mapped out distinct connections between personality patterns, body symbolism and health conditions. I find their books to be great sources of information for finding ideas and affirmations when I am creating my own healing chants.

Understanding Body Symbolism

I like to focus on the language we use to describe our bodies because these meanings are so clearly a part of our everyday consciousness and interactions. A single part of the body can be heavily laden with many different meanings. And sometimes the meanings are highly amusing as well.

For example, a "cheeky" person exhibits talk or behavior that is impertinent. A cheeky person is insolent, bold, cocky and disrespectful. On the other hand, to be "cheek to cheek" means "to be close and affectionate." To "turn the other cheek" is to be submissive or consciously chose not to retaliate. To be "tongue in cheek" is to poke fun and not take things too seriously.

Our digestive system is also full of contradictory meanings. Someone who is honest and emotionally vulnerable may be said to "spill their guts." We've all got "gut feelings" that warn us of impending danger. To go "belly up" is to go bankrupt. To "bust a gut" is to strain yourself, usually unnecessarily. If you can't let go of a problem or agitation about a situation or person, it's "eating you up." If you are constantly thinking about your problems, you are "contemplating your navel."

If you dislike someone, you just "can't stomach them." When you want to have more than you can handle, your "eyes are bigger than your stomach." And when you really dislike someone, you "hate their guts." That's pretty telling right there. We don't hate their kidneys or their forearms or their shoulders, we "hate their guts." The guts are the core of the person, both literally and symbolically.

Another part of the body highly laden with meaning is the feet. The feet represent the willingness to be on earth and engaged in life as in "putting your best foot forward." In contrast with this, someone who is afraid to rock the boat may be "walking on eggshells."

Feet represent our "understanding" of life. Your feet are literally "standing under" your body. Many chants have lyrics related to sitting at the feet of a spiritual master or deity.

Here's another fairly universal example: the shoulders represent the ability to carry our experiences and responsibilities in life. If we are so busy with what we "should" do, then our shoulders can become tense and rigid. A stiff or frozen shoulder may symbolize resistance to the pressure that life is exerting and an unwillingness to let others or life itself help us to carry the burden.

There are many songs in the repertoire of sacred music around the world about laying down our burdens. We can symbolically give our burdens over to a higher power such as a deity or life itself, potentially alleviating physical problems with the shoulders. Many chants emphasize surrender to a spiritual teacher or a representative of God. In any of these situations, a chant can be found or created that allows us to release our feelings into the physical world and potentially transform our physical bodies in a positive way.

Understanding the direct psychological connection between our physical bodies and our thoughts or emotions can help us to utilize the connection between chanting and the mind to heal the physical body. The patterns of our thoughts that have created discomfort or disease can be altered by choosing new thoughts and chanting them as mantras or sung affirmations.

Astrological Chants

I am not an expert in astrology, but I find the idea that life occurs in cycles to be reasonable and plausible. Those who have studied both astrology and mantras claim that the positive effects of astrological cycles can be accentuated and the negative effects can be ameliorated through chanting. Astrological chants are another potential avenue through which mantras can be used to enhance your life.

My personal connection to the stars in the heavens has always been more fundamental and childlike than learned. My father flew planes in the final years before flight navigation systems were computerized. He literally studied star maps and would determine his course by viewing or "shooting the stars" with handheld instruments.

As the seasons and constellations changed, he would have new, adjusted maps of the stars to study. He brought home the outdated star maps from work. Those were my first coloring books. As I traced the lines and constellations, I knew that I had come from somewhere out there. My home was among the stars! I learned the names of the stars and could point them out and recite their names in the night sky as a small child.

When I was five or six, my grandfather was building a house on a piece of land up on a mesa in New Mexico. Someone had practiced target shooting on the property with an old science textbook, which he brought home to me. I flipped through the book and found pictures of the solar system, complete with a bullet hole right through the middle. I could not understand how anyone could damage a book that contained a picture of the solar system. That seemed to me to be a desecration of something very holy. The universe, stars and heavenly bodies were always sacred to me.

What I love the most about using mantras in association with astrology is that they are purported to function like adaptogens. Adaptogens are herbs and plants that bring bodily functions into the normal range in either direction. If a system is overactive, they calm the system down. If a system or organ is underactive, they act as a stimulant.

The idea that chants act like adaptogens means that you don't have to know whether a particular planet is placed well in your chart to use astrological mantras. If the placement is good, the mantra will make things even better. If the placement is challenging, then the mantra will soothe and restore balance.

Surya

Sun Mantra

My favorite astrological chant is a chant to Surya, the Hindu god of the Sun. Surya is often depicted surrounded by the physical sun, riding in a chariot pulled by seven horses representing the seven chakras. His charioteer is Aruna. For me, this chant is the vocal equivalent of the Sun Salutation pose sequence often done in yoga classes.

A musical score for the following chant can be found in Chapter 21: Chants of Victory (p. 158).

> Om Bhaskaraya Vidmahe
> Om Maha Tejaya Dimahe
> Om Surya Namaha
> Om Surya Om
> Tanno Surya Prochodayat

The meaning of the Chant to the Sun is the following:

> Let me meditate on the Sun.
> Let me think about the highest power.
> I bow before the Sun.
> Homage to the Sun!
> Let the Giver of life illumine my mind."

Moon Mantra

The Sanskrit name of the moon is Chandra (see image below). Chandra's mantra is "Om Cam Chandraya Namah."

North Node of the Moon Mantra

The Sanskrit name for the North Node of the Moon is Rahu. The mantra is "Om Ram Rahave Namah."

South Node of the Moon Mantra

The Sanskrit name for the South Node of the Moon is Ketu. The mantra is "Om Kem Ketave Namah."

Chandra

Mars Mantra
The Sanskrit name of Mars is Kuja. The mantra is "Om Kum Kujaya Namah."

Mercury Mantra
The Sanskrit name of Mercury is Budha and the mantra is "Om Bum Budhaya Namah."

Jupiter Mantra
The Sanskrit name of Jupiter is Brihaspati and the mantra is "Om Brihaspataye Namah."

Venus Mantra
The Sanskrit name of Venus is Sukra and the mantra is "Om Sum Sukraya Namah."

Saturn Mantra
The Sanskrit name of Saturn is Sani and the mantra is "Om Sam Sanaye Namah."

Chapter 5
Sounds of the Cosmos

Some linguists believe that Sanskrit is closely related to onomatopoeia, the making of words aligned with the sound associated with what is named (cuckoo, sizzle, snap, splash). This is especially true of the bija mantras. The bija mantras are Sanskrit syllables that are said to correspond to specific meanings or aspects of creation and existence.

These words are often used individually or in combination with each other in mantras. Many are associated with specific goddesses in the Hindu tradition that are reputed to possess particular powers. The syllables can be correlated to energies in nature. They can also be thought of as aspects of our own divinity or distinct psychological traits.

OM (AUM): Causation
The Sanskrit word OM is familiar to most people as the quintessential mantra. OM is the fundamental mantra connecting us to higher reality and the highest aspect of our own beings. OM is believed to be a sound of the whole cosmic manifestation.

OM is the sound of the universe, the sound from which all other sounds are formed. OM represents past, present and future. OM is a seed or building block of creation.

OM can be viewed as having four parts: A-U-M followed by the sound of silence. The A (ahhh) represents the beginning, the connection to the physical world. The U (oooh) signifies the maintaining of the physical universe. The M (mmmm) is the transformative energy of the universe and the realm of thoughts and feelings. As noted, the fourth sound is the silence that follows the AUM. This is pure consciousness and knowingness.

OM represents both the manifest and unmanifest. In the form of AUM, this seed syllable is similar to the trinity of God in many other traditions. In that sense, the A represents Brahma or the Father; the U represents Vishnu, the Son or the preserver; and the M represents dissolution, the Holy Spirit or Shiva. OM is commonly associated solely with the latter (Shiva) as the cosmic masculine force.

OM is often included at the beginning of a mantra or chant to clear the mind for meditation. OM is said to draw the energy from the bottom of the spine to the top of the head. The energy of OM is one of expansion and ascension.

In terms of healing, OM brings prana into the subconscious mind. OM is the sound of the sun and sheds light on addictive tendencies and negative emotions, bringing them to light for healing and transmutation.

One of the simplest OM mantras is "OM, Shanti, Shanti, Shanti" meaning "OM, Peace, Peace, Peace."

AIM: Creation

AIM is the feminine counterpart of the bija mantra OM. The "AI" in AIM is pronounced "eye." AIM is a manifest form of OM, that which is created and seen versus that which is purely in consciousness. AIM is the supreme shakti or feminine force known as Adi Shakti. AIM appears in many mantras to the goddesses and the Divine Mother.

AIM is the seed mantra of Saraswati, goddess of knowledge, wisdom, music, art and speech. I view a seed mantra as the basic essence of an aspect of consciousness personified in a deity. Saraswati is revered in Hinduism, Jainism and some Buddhist sects. Her name means "one who leads to the essence of self-knowledge."

She has many beautiful names to acknowledge her many aspects. A few of these are the following:

- Saraswati Mata: Mother of Water and Lakes
- Bilvani Mata: Mother of the Woods
- Chandrika Mata: Mother of the Moon
- Hamsini Mata: Mother Who Rides the Swan
- Kadambari Mata: Mother of the Kadamba Flowers
- Malini Mata: Fragrant Mother
- Saradha Mata: Mother of the Harvest

AIM is also a general mantra for a higher knowledge and understanding. This can take the form of a guru or our own higher intelligence. AIM can help to orient us, motivate us and increase our will power to succeed.

In terms of physical healing, AIM strengthens the voice and vocal chords. Astrologically, AIM is related primarily to the moon and secondarily to the planet Mercury. An example of a mantra utilizing AIM is "OM AIM Saraswatyai Namaha."

HRIM: Divine Power

HRIM (hreem) is a mantra for the heart: the spiritual heart, the emotional heart and the physical heart. This mantra aids in longevity by energizing the heart. Due to the healing and stimulating influence on the heart, HRIM is also said to promote circulation and positively affects the lungs and nervous system.

HRIM is a combination of "ha" for prana and "ra" for fire and light with "ee" for focus and motivation. The sound HRIM may help us to connect with the deity of our choice at the level of the heart. This aids in allowing divine power to enter into our hearts. This bija mantra specifically relates to Parvati, the consort of Shiva. HRIM allows for both deep feeling and thought.

In Vedic astrology, HRIM relates to the sun, which is the planet of the heart. The solar energy and fire of the sun brings the outward expression of attraction and charisma. HRIM increases the finer energy of the heart. Conversely, HRIM can also be used harshly or negatively to mesmerize another person.

HRIM can be viewed as the prime mantra of all three shakti (feminine) powers: creation, preservation and destruction. HRIM can dissolve and carry away on the one hand and bring about joy and ecstasy on the other. In terms of the five elements, HRIM is mainly a fire mantra with some air element. An example of a mantra utilizing HRIM is "OM HRIM Parvati Mata."

HALIM: Protection

HALIM (hleem) is related to hrim. The fiery and stimulating "ra" sound is replaced with the "la." "La" is a water energy. This brings about a stabilizing and holding effect, often viewed as holding back negativity sent by others. HALIM is thought to bring water, earth and space together.

If HALIM is used gently, it is a mantra of bliss (ananda) and ecstasy. Used more forcefully, this seed sound can neutralize negativity. Used harshly, HALIM can destroy. HALIM can stop energy that has already been set in motion. Ideally, HALIM is the seed sound for protection.

HALIM relates to the goddess Bagalamukhi (bug-la-moo-key). This goddess is believed to seal the energy of an individual from negative outside influences, especially negative speech. Bagalamukhi is associated with the color yellow.

HALIM brings stillness through control of the body, mind, prana and senses. Turned inward, HALIM helps to stop inward chatter and is extremely useful for yoga and meditation. As such,

HALIM is a highly beneficial tool to reduce internal agitation.

Use HALIM with care—things can be brought to an abrupt halt. Chanting mantras for peace (shanti) to slow things down first is advised. From an astrological standpoint, HALIM is primarily related to Saturn and the north node of the moon (rahu) with a Mars influence. An example of a mantra utilizing HALIM is "OM HALIM Bagalamukhi, Sarva Buddha Bagalamukhi."

SHRIM: Growth and Surrender

SHRIM (shreem) brings positive growth and development. SHRIM attracts energy, situations and people who are beneficial for our lives. SHRIM is a mantra of surrender and devotion. SHRIM includes faith and refuge in a chosen aspect of God.

SHRIM is specifically the mantra of Lakshmi, the Hindu goddess of abundance and wealth. Lakshmi is the consort of Vishnu, the preserving aspect of the trinity. SHRIM can also be used in devotion to Rama. The literal meaning of SHRIM in Sanskrit is splendor. SHRIM is lunar whereas hrim is solar. SHRIM relates to the light of the moon and to the moon itself in Vedic astrology. SHRIM also connects to the beneficial aspects of Venus and Jupiter.

SHRIM is a watery and earthy mantra that is helpful for women's health and reproductive systems. SHRIM is soothing at all levels, bringing the type of surrender that allows for divine grace. HRIM is more related to the functional aspects of the heart while SHRIM is more closely associated with the feeling aspects of the heart.

An example of a mantra utilizing SHRIM is "OM HRIM SHRIM Lakshmi Bhayo Namaha" meaning "Lakshmi, reside in me and bestow thy abundance on all aspects of my existence."

KRIM: Divine Electricity

KRIM (kreem) is one of my favorite seed syllables. KRIM is a mantra of divine manifestation, specifically the divine electricity that exists behind all things. There is something about repeating this sound that really feels like a mild, positive electrical stimulus.

KRIM is the most important of the consonant mantras beginning with a hard consonant. The Sanskrit letter "k" or ka is an initial thrust of energy or prana. The letter "r" or ra adds fire and the "i" (ee) adds focus. KRIM is the Kriya Shakti or power of action that operates on all levels. The inner action is the awakening of the kundalini. KRIM also rules over time, helping us to move from past karma and master time, space and action.

KRIM is the seed mantra of the goddess Kali, known for her powers of transformation. She is a consort of Shiva and the feminine counterpart of his power of destruction. Kali is a personification of the power that frees us from all that would hinder our return to the highest vibration and Source energy.

KRIM is the mantra of yoga, allowing for inner concentration while outer action is taking place. This mantra connects to the inner power of the deity we have chosen to emphasize.

KRIM combines wind and electricity with fire. On the physical level, KRIM is like adrenaline. The circulatory and nervous systems are particularly affected as well as the heart and the liver.

Astrologically, KRIM relates primarily to the planet Mars, the planet of work and effort. KRIM can be harsh or strong and should be recited with care. An example of a mantra utilizing KRIM is "OM KRIM Kalikayai Namaha" which calls the energy of Kali and her power into action in the world.

KLIM: Divine Magnetism

KLIM (kleem) is a softer counterpart to "krim." Rather than projecting energy and electricity outward, KLIM draws all towards itself with a type of divine magnetism. KLIM carries the shakti power of attraction and is said to help hold or fix things in place like gravity.

KLIM can be used related to any deity, but is particularly associated with Krishna, Sundari (Lalita) and the softer forms of Kali or Durga. As the seed mantra of attraction and desire, KLIM helps us to achieve our true desires in life.

KLIM helps to increase love and devotion. It is a heart-focused mantra that is safe to use liberally. This makes KLIM one of the most widely used mantras among the bija seed syllables. KLIM brings divine love and beauty into our surroundings and our lives. KLIM is mainly associated with the water element and is helpful for the skin and body fluids such as digestive fluids as well as the reproductive system. KLIM helps to increase our capacity to absorb nourishment. KLIM strengthens the immune system and brings contentment on an emotional level.

An example of a mantra utilizing KLIM is "OM AIM HRIM KLIM Chamundaye Viche" which calls to Durga and removes negativity of all kinds.

DUM: Divine Salvation

DUM (duhm) is a mantra of divine salvation: a combination of protection and self-discipline. This is the mantra of Durga, who saves us from difficulties whenever possible. Durga leads a divine army and rides a lion.

This is a powerful fire mantra with a weapon-like effect. DUM is an earthly fire rather than an etheric fire. The martial energy of DUM overcomes opposition and is also a transformative energy to eliminate sorrow and obstacles both within and without. DUM grants self-control.

DUM with a long vowel (pronounced doom) is similar but softer and more feminine. This form of DUM also neutralizes negative forces projected against us. DUM is beneficial for tissues in the body and can be used to burn away toxins and also to increase the digestive fire. DUM is a solar energy. An example of a mantra utilizing DUM is "Ma Durga DUM Durgayei Namaha," which is a mantra combining protection and self-discipline.

There is something about singing a chant with the word DUM used repeatedly that makes me feel like a toddler beating on pots and pans on the kitchen floor. Using mantras or any other tools to consciously change our own emotional or psychological patterns can be a serious thing, yet DUM feels more like play.

HUM: Divine Fire

HUM (huhm) is a fire mantra that can help to kindle the consciousness. This is an etheric fire connected to lightning, pranic fire, and the breath. This lightning can also be used for protection. HUM is sometimes referred to as the "seed syllable of wrath" or righteous anger.

HUM is the mantra that Shiva projects from his third eye to destroy all negativity and burn up all human desires. HUM is connected closely to the transformative power of the trinity. HUM with a long vowel (pronounced hoom) is slightly softer and related to fierce goddesses like Kali and Chandi.

Chandi is a personification of one of the shakti powers of Brahma. The name "Chandi" means "she who tears apart thought." Chandi proclaims her preeminence as both the formless and the formed universe. This specific form of her power is more like a sword versus lightning.

HUM with the long vowel also has a wooing characteristic, like the sound of a cow calling to her calf. In this form it is both invocative and protective.

HUM is focused in the navel area and digestive fire as well as the fire of the mind. Both the long and short forms of HUM can strengthen the immune system to ward off pathogenic attacks.

Astrologically, the forms of HUM are related to fiery planets like the Sun and Mars or Ketu (the south lunar node). An example of a mantra utilizing HUM is "Maha Shakti Chandi Shakti HUM" meaning "Praise to Mother Chandi who protects me with her fire." This mantra can also be used to create a protective forcefield around a dwelling.

I had an experience of this sense of protection one night when I woke up about 2 am and felt a bit shaken, the way you feel when waking up from a bad dream. I didn't consciously try to figure out what chant was right for the situation, but the Chandi mantra came to mind. I got up and chanted for an hour or so. I don't know if that particular chant made a difference or if the effect was just from chanting itself, but I was grateful to sleep soundly after that.

PART II
Transformation and the Chakras

Chapter 6
Wheels of Fire:
The Seven Chakras

I was taking a swing dance class with my husband several years ago. He was very enthusiastic about having me there as he was an avid ballroom dancer at the time. I was less keen on attending. However, I had agreed to go in the spirit of a shared activity. There were twenty or thirty people in the class and the men were lined up in a circle around the edge of the room.

The women would dance with one man for a moment or two, practicing a variety of spinning moves, and then move on to the next man and repeat the same steps and spins. We were nearing the end of the hour. Since we were repeating the same spins over and over, we were actually whirling around much more than one normally would in an actual dance.

Suddenly I felt a rushing sense like a campfire ignited at the base of my spine, instantaneously filling my pelvis and beginning to move upwards. I had never experienced that kind of thing before but had read and studied enough to recognize what was happening. I knew it had something to do with the kundalini energy at the base of the spine beginning to rise. However, I had no clue what would happen next.

I was panicked about being in a public place during this unusual experience. Was I going to have a seizure? Would I fall to the floor twitching and writhing and humiliate myself? Would

I loseconsciousness? Would they have to call an ambulance for me? "No!" I commanded instantly, "Not here! Not now!" The experience ended as quickly as it had begun. I walked to the foyer, changed my shoes and headed for the car. To my husband's great disappointment, I refused to take any more dance classes.

Afterward, I did some research into the whirling dervish dances of the Sufis, which seemed to be the closest thing to what I had experienced. The whirling dervishes and even Tibetan prayer wheels are based on the principle that rotational force can result in energy rising upward. Interestingly, children often play a game of spinning around until they are too dizzy to stand up. As adults, we are generally moving only forwards or backwards.

Understanding the Kundalini

What I experienced seems to have been a form of spontaneous kundalini movement. The Sanskrit word "kundalini" means "coiled like a snake." The snake is a common symbol of the kundalini, an energy curled at the base of the spine. As the kundalini moves upward, the energy flows through seven major energy centers called chakras.

Many mystics and yogis have written and taught about the rising of the kundalini. In many traditions, bringing the energy to the crown of the head is considered to be the physical counterpart to achieving enlightenment. Of course, some mystics have achieved elevated states without any knowledge of such things, and you do not have to know about the kundalini or the chakras to chant. All the same, if you either want to cultivate this consciously or you have any spontaneous experiences, familiarity with these things could be helpful.

There are many approaches to awakening and raising the kundalini. A wide variety of ancient and modern meditation and yoga practices can guide you in that direction if desired. Even non-spiritual practices can be effective. For example, Dr. Francis Lefebure, a French physician and scientist (1916-1988), designed a device called a Gyrascope that would awaken the kundalini when used for about an hour a day.

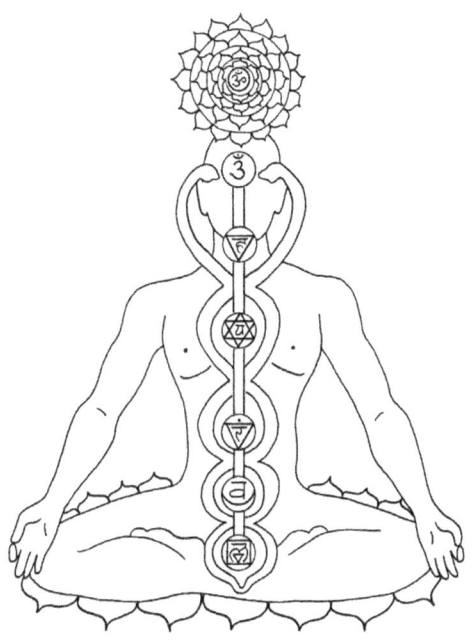

Understanding the Chakras

Although most sources describe seven chakras, there may be many more than seven energy centers in the body. Some systems include eight chakras (adding a sub-chakra for the heart called the secret chamber of the heart). Other systems include twelve chakras (adding chakras in the hands and feet and one in the side). Other systems include one hundred forty-four chakras or more.

The colors associated with the chakras also differ in various traditions. Many systems use the colors of the rainbow. Others use a sequence of white, violet, purple/gold, pink, blue, green, and yellow, beginning at the base and moving up to the crown chakra.

This second set of colors are purported to be the purified colors of the chakras or the chakras in their etheric state. Personally, I prefer to use this second system of colors.

Illustrations of the chakras often include extensive symbolism, Sanskrit letters, and hieroglyphs. They are a study in ancient wisdom and spirituality, recording various aspects of consciousness associated with each chakra. There are a number of ways to understand and work with the chakras. Among these are:

- toning the seed syllables or primordial sounds for each of the seven chakras
- chanting mantras dedicated to the deities associated with each chakra
- visualizing light and healing for the physical organs associated with each chakra
- working with the psychological and emotional aspects of each chakra
- using visualizations, yantras (sacred art) and color therapy for the chakras
- using essential oils and healing stones for the chakras

There are differences in the recommendations from source to source for these approaches. Research and personal experience will help you to determine which tools are most helpful for you. Although I like to practice the seed syllables for each chakra and I do think about the chakras associated with various deities in many cases, this is not always in the forefront of my mind when I am chanting. I find the understanding of chakras to be helpful and useful. At the same time, the intention to use chanting to serve life and increase my own ability to love is my primary consideration.

Also, please be aware that these tools can be powerful. In the process of healing, clearing and balancing the chakras with chanting and other tools, memories and emotions can be released.

For example, if you practice any of these approaches to working with the chakras regularly, you may suddenly feel grief or anger rather than elation or bliss. If this occurs, please take care of yourself. Get the assistance you may need from family, friends and professionals. In the end, this is all energy. In my experience, the key is to transform the energy rather than to deny or suppress emerging feelings.

Clearly my own favorite practice for balancing and healing the chakras and transforming energy is chanting. Other practices that I have found to be successful include exercise, meditation and journaling. You will likely want to use a combination of approaches that work for your temperament and personality.

Understanding Hindu Deities

For me, the Hindu deities represent aspects of consciousness. Ultimately it seems that we will reach a state where we experience ourselves as part of everything that is in existence and part of every possible mental, emotional and psychological state. For this reason, my personal view is that the multiplicity of deities in Hinduism is not in conflict with monotheism. In fact, the pantheon of Hindu gods are reminiscent of the many Catholic saints of my childhood.

When I was being confirmed in the Catholic church as a young teenager, I took the choice of a confirmation name very seriously. I borrowed books from the parish library and read the lives of the saints to find one I wanted to emulate. Each saint had unique characteristics and a particular aspect of God that was their speciality. Many of the lives of the saints were quite dramatic, sometimes even bizarre. The feats they performed and the miracles associated with them made them feel superhuman to me.

These stories of saints were similar to the mythologies associated with Hindu deities. In addition, sometimes the Hindu deities are an intense mix of godlike qualities and seemingly very human attributes including jealousy, envy, revenge and so forth. Perhaps this is even closer to classical mythology and the heroes and heroines of the Greeks and Romans rather than Catholic saints. In any case, I don't mind that the gods and goddesses sometimes seem less than holy. They are passionately alive. Perhaps they are sometimes mistaken but they are never lukewarm. I appreciate that. Living with confidence and fearlessness is worth a misstep now and then.

In the end, my experience has been that the most empowering approach is to ask myself what qualities I need to develop to be a more complete human being. Do I need to be ruthless in separating myself from a victim mentality? Do I need to care less what others think and pursue my own path with more power and directness? Do I need to clarify my goals and be a better example of adventurous living for my children? Do I need to soften and treat others with greater patience?

Which deity best exemplifies the qualities that I need to embody? What are the qualities associated with Kali or Parvati or Hanuman or any of the other deities? My chants are really a way to develop those qualities within myself rather than worship them in an external being. I like to know the meaning of the chants I sing and to be conscious of my intent. My hope is that if I become more clear, more compassionate, more powerful, more loving and more whole as a human being, then becoming more godlike will take care of itself.

CHAPTER 7
Establishing Safety: Base Chakra

The name for the root or base chakra in Sanskrit is the Muladhara. This is the chakra of safety and security. "Mula" means "root" and "adhara" means "base or support." This chakra is at the base of the spine and can be viewed as establishing your connection to your physical body, the earth, and the environment. The base chakra is associated with survival instincts for food, shelter, safety, comfort and belonging.

Muladhara Chakra

Most sources say that the base chakra governs the lower part of the body, including the legs, hips, lower back and lower spine. The physical organs associated with the base chakra are the feet, the little (baby) toes, the knees, the pelvis, the little (baby) fingers, the skeletal system and the muscular system. These are generally the organs and systems that provide a strong foundation for physical health and a platform for our presence in the world.

In the Hindu tradition, the base chakra is depicted as a lotus flower with four petals. Each of the petals represent one of the mental states associated with this chakra. The interpretations and translations of the meaning associated with each of these petals vary widely.

Some of the variations may be due to the difficulty of translating directly from Sanskrit, a language that assigns many meanings to a single word. Of course this is common in other languages as well (thus the term homonymns).

However, having multiple meanings for a single word is so prolific in Sanskrit that the term polysemy is more appropriate. Polysemy means that many, many related terms can be associated with a single word. Polysemy leads to sets and subsets of related meanings so that the judgments needed to determine the exact meaning of a word in a particular context can be difficult to make.

Generally, the four petals of the base chakra are viewed as mind, intellect, consciousness and ego. Alternately, the petals can represent four forms of longing: dharma (psychological longing), artha (soul longing), kama (physical longing) and moksha (longing for spiritual liberation). These petals are also symbolic of four specific aspects of higher consciousness: great joy, natural pleasure, delight in controlling passion, and blissfulness in concentration.

All of this can be a bit heavy, philosophical and theoretical. As a highly visual person, I simply find delight in the grace and beauty of the Hindu symbols for the chakras. I like the balance of simplicity and complexity. I appreciate the attempts of ancient and modern artists to depict energy patterns which may be very real but are unseen and unproven for most of us.

Most interpretations of the typical Hindu symbol for the base chakra are that the central square represents stability. This chakra provides the foundation upon which the other chakras rest.

The upside-down triangle is an alchemical symbol for the earth, often interpreted as a grounded energy. The base chakra is often associated with the color red, but in a higher form this chakra may emit the white energy of the kundalini or Mother light.

The base chakra can be seen as connected with your personal and ancestral history. These are the roots that can either bind you to the earth in a negative sense or give you a strong base and presence in the world. A balanced and strong base chakra affords the ability to stand your ground and feel safe in the world.

The base chakra is related to establishing a foundation of basic security in your environment and social world. I had lots of opportunities as a kid to reestablish that base and foundation in my life. Growing up in the military, we moved regularly. By the time I graduated from high school, I had been in ten schools.

I noticed as I got older that the other military kids tended to be more outgoing than the kids who had remained in the same geographic region all of their lives. It was easy to find and make friends with the other military kids wherever we went. They, too, knew what it was like to be the new kid over and over again. I suppose we had to learn to have an inner foundation to be adaptable repeatedly in new situations.

Deities and Chants for the Base Chakra

The deities Indra, Brahma and Ganesha are associated with the base chakra. These deities help to establish a foundation: Brahma is the creative aspect of God, Indra belongs to the heaven above, and Ganesha helps to overcome obstacles here on earth. For this reason, Ganesha is often invoked in the beginning of a practical endeavor.

Indra

Indra is the king of heaven. He is associated with lighting, thunder, storms, rain and rivers. Indra rides on a elephant, symbolizing compassion, intelligence and ancient wisdom. An elephant with seven trunks is sometimes depicted, representing all seven of the major chakras or energy centers in the body.

Indra

Brahma

Brahma is the Hindu creator god also known as the Self-Born, the Lord of Speech, and the creator of the four Vedas. Brahma is the consort of Saraswati, the goddess of knowledge and wisdom.

Brahma is traditionally depicted with four faces and four arms. Each face points to a cardinal direction. His hands hold symbols of knowledge and creation: sacred texts, mala beads symbolizing time, a ladle used to feed a sacrificial fire, and a lotus.

Brahma is often depicted with a white beard and a sage-like expression. He sits on a lotus flower, dressed in white, red or pink, often with a swan or goose nearby upon which he can ride.

Ganesha

Ganesha is often invoked at the beginning of an undertaking or an event. Ganesha is also a patron of writers and learning. Ganesha became a popular deity in the 2nd to 5th centuries AD. He is found in various traditions including Jainism and Buddhism.

Ganesha

Ganesha is the son of Parvati and Shiva but was created by Parvati independently. This resulted in confusion for Shiva, who returned after a long absence, did not know his own son and mistakenly cut off his son's head. This was a huge obstacle in his relationship with Parvati.

To remedy this error, he placed the head of an elephant on his son's body and magically fused the head in place to save his son's life. His son became known as Ganesha, the remover of obstacles.

The following is a chant to Ganesha:

> Ganesha Sharanam Sharanam Ganesha
> Ganesha Sharanam Sharanam Ganesha
> Sayisha Sharanam Sharanam Ganesha Sharanam
> Sayisha Sharanam Sharanam Ganesha Sharanam

This chant means "I take refuge (sayisha) in Ganesha. I surrender (sharanam) to Ganesha." I think of this as meaning: "I surrender all within myself that would interfere with the successful completion of this undertaking."

CHAPTER 8
Healing Relationships: Sacral Chakra

The second or sacral chakra is known as Svadhishthana. This chakra is the seat of the self and the relationship of the self with others. The organs associated with the sacral chakra are the reproductive organs, the kidneys and the bladder.

The six petals of the sacral chakra are associated with the syllables ban, bham, mam, yam, ram and lam. These syllables

Svadhishthana Chakra

can be interpreted as desirable modes of consciousness or as the overcoming of undesirable modes of consciousness. In the center is a white crescent moon representing water energy and the emotions. The sacral chakra is said to house the unconscious. This is sometimes symbolized as the ocean.

The sacral chakra is also the seat of creation, sometimes called the seat of the soul. My own greatest awareness of the sacral chakra was during my first two pregnancies. When I got married in my late twenties, I was not sure that I could have children at all. I had had a long history of highly irregular periods. By the time I was thirty, I had been trying to get pregnant for three years.

I had gone through multiple types of fertility treatments. They were painful, inconvenient, expensive and unfruitful. Yet I had wanted a large family from early childhood. I was struggling with the heartache of thinking that the reality of a family might never come to pass. Still, my body was not responding well. I stopped pursuing the various treatments.

One morning a few months later, I was at work and suddenly felt such a tremendous joy, so distinct and remarkable that I called my husband to say, "I don't know what just happened, but I feel incredibly happy!"

I didn't connect it at that moment to conceiving a child since conception often takes place one to two days after intimate relations. I remembered that deep sense of joy about ten days later when I found out that I was indeed pregnant. I felt very close to my daughter throughout the pregnancy.

About a year and a half after my daughter's birth, we wanted to expand our family and I was staying alert for the same kind of experience indicating a second conception. At the time my daughter attended a daycare center while I worked. I went there to have lunch with her.

I was sitting at the lunch table with her and suddenly felt a shower of light so physical I could almost see it all around me. The feeling was like standing under a waterfall. I knew instantly that I had conceived another child and looked at the clock to mark the time.

With our third, fourth and fifth children, I was so busy caring for the older ones and helping my husband run a multimedia business that I was less conscious of the conceptions, though I felt very close to each child throughout those pregnancies.

Deities and Chants for the Sacral Chakra

The sacral chakra is associated with the deity Vishnu and the goddess Parvati. There are others, but these are two of the main sacral chakra deities. Parvati, also known as Uma, is the Hindu goddess of fertility, love and devotion as well as divine strength and power. She is the gentle and nurturing aspect of the goddess energy.

Parvati

Parvati is part of a trinity of Hindu goddesses that also includes Lakshmi, the goddess of wealth and prosperity, and Saraswati, the goddess of knowledge and learning. Parvati is the consort of Shiva and the mother of Ganesha and Kartikeya. She is the daughter of Himavan (the god and personification of the Himalayas) and Queen Mena. Parvati's name is derived from the Sanskrit words for "mountain" and can be translated as "daughter of the mountains." The following is a chant to Parvati:

> Parvati Parashakti Parvati
> Jai Parvati Shakti Mata

This chant means "Praise and honor to Parvati, the highest expression of God as Mother!"

CHAPTER 9
Honoring Intuition: Solar Plexus Chakra

The third chakra or solar plexus chakra is known as Manipura. The name translates as the "city of jewels." "Mani" means "gem" while "pura" means "city." When purified, this is the chakra of inner peace. The solar plexus chakra is located at the naval, center of intuition (a gut feeling). This chakra is connected to both service and desires. This is the chakra where we get a gut feeling about people, places and events.

Manipura Chakra

This chakra governs the power of transformation. In the physical realm, this is digestion, pancreatic function, the liver, the large intestines, the stomach and adrenal function. This chakra is the center of digestion for food as well as the digestion of thoughts and emotions. The solar plexus is the fire center, often symbolized by the colors yellow or red and a sun-like image.

Manipura is represented as a ten-petaled lotus bearing the Sanskrit letters da, dha, na, ta, tha, da, dha, na, pa, and pha. These petals correspond to the overcoming of spiritual ignorance, thirst, jealousy, treachery, shame, fear, disgust, delusion, foolishness and sadness.

I learned the importance of listening to my gut at a point in my life when I was collaborating with someone on a large creative project. It was a test project and we planned to duplicate the idea on a much larger scale if the pilot project was successful. This project was one of those ideas and possibilities that just made my heart leap for joy. My partner in the project appeared to have a commitment as deep as mine. Yet I simultaneously had a growing sense of anxiety at the core of my being. My heart and gut were clearly in conflict. I found the experience to be confusing and distressing.

Sure enough, my associate suddenly and inexplicably changed directions. Communication stopped. My attempts to reach out were rebuffed. My colleague no longer wanted to keep to our timelines: there were other projects, plans and activities aside from our joint efforts that were now taking priority.

At first, I was devastated. I had invested a significant amount of money, endless hours of discussion, and lots of psychological and emotional energy in the partnership and in the long-term vision we had together. At the same time, I had never experienced such a deep division within my own being along the way: great excitement and heart-felt enthusiasm combined with deep gut-level concern and warning.

I began to analyze the situation to determine which elements of the partnership had been successful in spite of the abrupt ending and which aspects of the project I could continue to pursue independently. That approach was a great comfort.

A few months later I came across the concept of the three brains. I first heard the concept in a podcast between the actor and comedian Russell Brand and Ed Stafford, a survivalist, adventurer and author of *Walking the Amazon.* Stafford attributes the concept of the three brains to a discussion he had with one of the native people that befriended him during his travels.

According to this indigenous approach, the first brain is the thinking brain. In the western world, we have historically given prominence to the thinking brain: I think, therefore I am. Our emphasis on academics and rationality and logicality reflect this approach. The second brain is the heart. As a society, we have tried to shift to heart-centered living in more recent times. We tell our children to "follow their hearts." Preschoolers sing songs with words like "my heart tells me what to do." This is a step in a more holistic direction.

The third brain is the gut. Until my experience with the discontinued plans, I would have attributed a gut-level feeling of anxiety to my own limitations and fears getting in the way of moving forward. After all, we are supposed to be going out of our comfort zones, right? I thought I had to overcome my anxiety by an act of will and kept pushing ahead for the stated goal.

Now I have come to view the messages from my gut as communications from my soul. The soul seems to have a way of getting a bearing on what is unforeseen, or perhaps notices the red flags that we choose to ignore. I have a new cascading hierarchy for decision-making. If the thinking brain and heart are in conflict, follow the heart. If the heart and soul are in conflict, follow the soul. This is the beauty and importance of messages and feelings originating in the solar plexus chakra.

Deities and Chants for the Solar Plexus Chakra

One of the Hindu deities associated with the solar plexus chakra is Lakshmi, well-known as the goddess of wealth, fortune and prosperity. Lakshmi also appears as a deity in Jainism and Buddhism. Lakshmi is endowed with six auspicious or divine qualities known as gunas. In one story, Lakshmi is born from Prajapati, the Lord of all creatures. The gods become covetous of her and demand that she be killed so that they can take her powers. Prajapati refuses and says that the other gods must seek her gifts without violence. Lakshmi's gifts include imperial authority, martial energy, priestly authority, dominion, splendor and nourishment. The following is a chant to Lakshmi:

Om Hrim Shrim Lakshmi Bhayo Namaha

The meaning of this chant can be understood as follows: Hrim invokes prana, light, fire and space and brings about joy, longevity and rejuvenation. Shrim promotes positive growth and enlightenment. This is the seed syllable of Lakshmi herself.

Lakshmi

CHAPTER 10
Giving Devotion: Heart Chakra

The fourth chakra is the heart chakra or the Anahata chakra. In Sanskrit, "Anahata" means "unhurt, unstruck, unbeaten." At the same time, Anahata means "pure" or "clean." The physical organs associated with the heart chakra are the heart itself, the circulatory system and the lungs.

As the seat of love and devotion, the heart expresses charity, compassion, and kindness. The heart is also a focus for beauty

Anahata Chakra

and culture. The energy of this chakra integrates opposite forces or brings two parts together. The heart chakra is symbolized by a twelve-petaled lotus with interlocking triangles in the center. This is a depiction of yin and yang or male and female.

My own experiences related to the heart chakra have intensified over the last few years. This seems to be directly related to the heart-opening practice of chanting. For example, I have started experiencing a distinct sensation of burning in my heart. I am learning to take note of whatever is happening when this occurs.

As a result, I have started to navigate through life in a new way. In addition to paying more attention to my gut feelings, I determine my course of action in life as much as possible based on this burning sensation in my heart.

I remember exactly when I started guiding my life in this way. One day just before I made the decision to start leading kirtan, I was sitting in a car with a friend after a beautiful walk along a river here in Montana. We had been talking for an hour or more, catching up with each other's lives and children and so forth.

Just as I was about to get out of the car to go home, she began to talk about a conference she had attended led by a sound healer. Immediately I felt my heart burning. This was important! In those final moments of our visit, I asked her for all the information I needed to pursue whatever I could learn from that particular method of sound healing.

Although I had always known that my life's mission was related to transformation through science, psychology and the arts, I have found the process of deciding what training and experiences I needed to pursue in that regard to be overwhelming. After my experience talking to my friend, I stayed on the alert for the sensation of burning in my heart. To be really reliable, this heart-felt sensation had to be combined with a sense of peace–or at least an absence of anxiety–in my solar plexus.

With this approach, life becomes a bit like the hot/cold party game. Something is hidden and one or more people are guided in their search by the responses of someone who knows where the item is located: "Cold, cold, cold, lukewarm, hot, hotter, burning hot!" until the item is found.

I think the heart chakra functions like a spiritual GPS, always leading us to our own true north. There is really no fear of getting lost or going astray. If we turn into a byway or take a detour, our heart simply recalculates the path instantly.

Deities and Chants for the Heart Chakra

Hanuman is a key deity in the Hindu tradition associated with the heart chakra. Hanuman is the monkey god, hero of epics and stories in Hinduism, Jainism and Buddhism. Hanuman is the ardent devotee of Lord Rama, and he plays a central role in the epic poem *Ramayana*.

Hanuman is sometimes depicted as the patron of martial arts, wrestling, and acrobatics. I think of Hanuman as an Eastern

Hanuman

superhero, somewhat akin to Superman or Spiderman or Batman. He is also the patron of meditation and scholarship.

The powers of Hanuman include the following:

- cannot be killed with any weapon in war
- power to induce fear in enemies
- power to destroy fear in friends
- cannot be harmed by lightning
- cannot be drowned (protection from water)
- cannot be harmed by fire
- can make himself as small or as large as he wants
- will always be happy and content

Some interpretations of the name Hanuman are based on the fact that the Sanskrit word "han" means "killed or destroyed" and "maana" means "pride." Therefore the name would mean "one whose pride was destroyed."

Chants to Hanuman tend to be joyful and fun. Hanuman The following is an example of a chant to Hanuman:

> Hanuman Bolo, Jaya Sita Ram
> Jaya Sita Ram Hanuman
> Hanuman Bolo, Hanuman Bolo,
> Jaya Sita Ram Jay Jay Hanuman

The word "bolo" means "I sing." This chant means "I sing of Hanuman! Victory to Sita and Ram! Victory to Hanuman!"

Chapter 11
Mastering Power: Throat Chakra

The fifth chakra is the throat chakra or the Vishuddha chakra. In Sanskrit, Vishuddha means "especially pure." The throat chakra is depicted as having sixteen petals. In the center is a triangle pointing downward and a white circle representing akashi or ether. The throat chakra is associated with creativity and self-expression as well as the actions of speaking and chanting.

Vishuddha Chakra

This chakra is associated with the neck, the esophagus, the teeth, the mouth and the ears.

When I first began chanting, I had been on thyroid medication for over twenty years. The thyroid is the largest organ associated directly with the throat. According to many esoteric teachings, the throat is the seat of power and creativity. The throat and thyroid are where emotions, intentions, praise and criticism are expressed.

My extended family has struggled with thyroid issues for generations. My paternal grandmother had a goiter, an abnormal growth of the thyroid. My maternal grandmother had hyperthyroidism, an overly active thyroid. This was treated with oblation, which is full or partial destruction of the thyroid, followed by lifelong medication. Both hypothyroidism (low thyroid) and hyperthyroidism are present in my immediate family. Perhaps my genetics for this particular organ are not ideal.

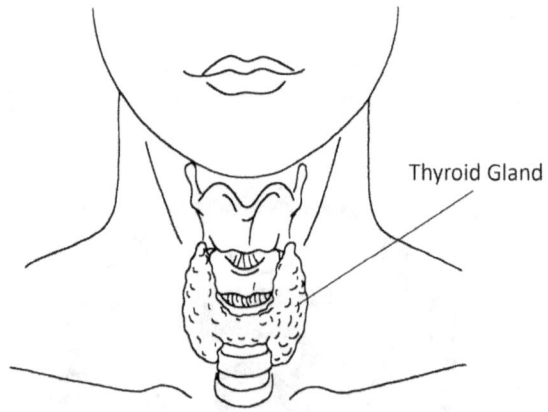

There is a legend that goes as follows: when the human body was being created, God was trying to figure out where to hide the power center so that man would not misuse this fundamental energy. So He hid the power center in plain sight in the throat— a place where man would qualify this fundamental energy for blessing or bane with every word spoken.

The throat is the place of greatest vulnerability and greatest strength. This is revealed in many common expressions. To attack someone else with lethal intent is to "go for the throat." To be deeply moved by unexpressed grief or sadness is to have "a lump in your throat." To be self-destructive is to "cut your own throat." To be forced to do something unwillingly is to have something "shoved down your throat." To put forth great effort is to "grab something by the throat."

To maintain the thyroid in balance, we have to have a balanced ability to speak up for ourselves without causing harm to others. Setting appropriate boundaries with others is a way to do this. This is particularly challenging for women, who tend to take the role of assisting others no matter what the cost to themselves.

If you haven't spoken up for yourself in years, you may find that you have a lot to say. When I began to do this for myself, much of what I had to say had to first be expressed in a journal so that it could be completely unfiltered (and then burned). I would also have conversations out loud by imagining that people from my past and present were sitting in front of me. I got the chance to say what I wished I could have said. Sometimes my conversations with the ghosts of my earlier life were quite heated. Other times they were extremely emotional. Often they were very sad.

I also made practical changes in my life. I wanted to find ways to have a greater sense of personal power, something I thought would benefit my throat chakra and thyroid. For example, rather than having all of my income contributing solely to the support of my family, I established my own checking and savings accounts and got a credit card in my name alone.

My husband and I established a budget for the household and we each began to contribute equally. Any money earned beyond that would be for each of us to spend or save as desired for ourselves.

I also decided that I wanted to have a car in my own name. At that time my family (which included several drivers in their teens and early twenties) had a small fleet of old cars that were jointly owned or driven by whoever needed transportation on a given day. Having a vehicle in my own name was largely symbolic, but the sense of ownership mattered to me.

In addition, my working life for a long time had consisted of doing whatever was necessary to pay the bills. I ran a multimedia company with my husband. We did everything from websites to book layouts to commercials and radio spots.

Most of my time was spent in administrative tasks, project management and client communications rather than the creative side of the business. Over the years our multimedia business became successful, but the stress of supporting our family solely through self-employment was notable.

I was also a professional artist and a piano teacher, which are creative endeavors that would allow for activation of the throat chakra. However, in the early years of our business those jobs were part-time and did not earn a sufficient living. While I was working on healing my thyroid, my husband decided to take a full-time job with our largest client. This gave me the opportunity to be the sole owner of our business and gradually focus my working life on the things that matter the most to me: devotional music, sacred art, and understanding the process of transformation of the spirit, mind and body.

During the most intensive period of working consciously on healing my thyroid and throat chakra, I also started weight lifting with my youngest son. If you want a sense of personal power, body building is a fantastic tool. I had a blast and gained in both confidence and strength.

I wanted to give some further support to my thyroid on the physical level. This was a long-term, fairly serious medical condition. I used a natural supplement of glandular extracts, herbs, amino acids, minerals and essential oils for a few months. I gradually weaned myself off thyroid medication with my doctor's supervision and blood testing as necessary to make sure my thyroid levels were acceptable.

In combination with these practical measures, chanting was an ideal tool, since the vibrations of chanting and singing pass directly through the thyroid gland. Chanting gave me practice in sending energy and healing through my throat chakra. Besides the Sanskrit chants included below (see Deities and Chants for the Throat Chakra), I created my own chants in English using healing affirmations focused on personal power in a healthy and joyful way.

One of my chants was sung to the tune of "Row, Row, Row Your Boat" and went something like this: "I feel power flow every day through me! Power for healing and power for feeling, and I live merrily!"

Perhaps that seems silly. I didn't care as long as I was getting results. Chanting was a way to shift my approach to life: literally making noise and making changes versus remaining quietly accepting of circumstances around me and of limitations in my own well-being.

Healing my thyroid took conscious effort on many levels. I had tried to heal this condition in the past without success. I believe that adding the practice of chanting was a crucial component in finally alleviating this condition.

Today I no longer have the symptoms of low thyroid that used to plague me even when I was on moderate to high doses of medication. Gone are the days of dry skin. Gone are the days of having cold feet and hands. Gone are the days of being tired only hours after awakening. Gone is the sense of being weighed down by life.

This process took many months, probably a year or more from start to finish, but was well worth the effort. Chanting has been both a catalyst and a means to a healthier life and body. I am immensely grateful.

Please work closely with your health practitioner if you make lifestyle changes that may affect your health in any way. Be gentle with yourself. Dramatic positive changes are possible, but slow, steady improvements may be easier to handle. I have developed patience (not a natural trait for me) and persistence through this process of healing. Chanting is a fantastic part of a holistic approach to living life to your fullest potential.

Deities and Chants for the Throat Chakra

There are specific sounds that are precisely connected to the throat chakra. One of these is the syllable "ham" (pronounced hum).

The simplest mantra for the throat and thyroid is "Om Ham Namaha." This means something like: "I bow and give honor to the power of God within my throat chakra." This works on both the spiritual and physical levels.

The presiding deity for the throat chakra is Panchavaktra Shiva or Sadashiva. This is Shiva, the third member of the Hindu trinity, in all five of his major forms: Aghora, Ishana, Tat Purusha, Vamadeva (Varna Deva) and Rudra.

The prefix sada in the name Sadashiva means "always" or "forever." Sadashiva is the one who is always happy, loving and auspicious. Sadashiva is the core of deep happiness that exists even in the midst of suffering.

Sadashiva is sometimes depicted as having five faces and ten arms. The consort of Sadashiva is the goddess Gayatri or Adishakti. In the Hindu tradition, Shiva is known as the destroyer of all that is unreal. The following is one of my favorite chants to Sadashiva:

> Namo Sadashiva Shambo
> Hey Shiva Shankara Shambo
> Namo Sadashiva Shambo
> Hey Shiva Shankara Shambo
> Bhagavan Deva Shiva Shambo
> Sadashiva Deva Shiva Shambo
> Bhagavan Deva Shiva Shambo
> Sadashiva Deva Shiva Shambo

"Namo" means "I bow." "Bhagavan" means "Lord," often used in reference to Krishna or Shiva, and implies that someone is glorious, fortunate, or blessed. "Shambo" means "abode of joy." Deva is a masculine noun denoting divinity.

11 | Mastering Power: Throat Chakra

Sadashiva

Chapter 12
Holding a Vision: Third Eye Chakra

The sixth chakra is the third eye, the seat of spiritual vision. The Sanskrit term for this chakra is Ajna, which means "command" or "perceive." The pineal gland or third eye is associated with this chakra. The third eye, usually associated with clairvoyant abilities, can be developed with yoga, meditation and the practice of chanting. The vibrations of chanting and singing are felt in the skull and can be consciously directed to the third eye. Other physical organs associated with the third eye are the eyes, the ears and the pituitary gland.

Ajna Chakra

The superficial location of the third eye is between the eyebrows at the bridge of the nose. This sacred spot is sometimes marked in the East on the forehead by the red dot known as the bindi. The third eye is the door to prophetic vision and seeing the future.

The third eye is associated with several deities and combined forms of deities. Shiva as Tryambaka Deva is often depicted as having three eyes. Other deities associated with the third eye include Vishnu, the Sustainer, and his incarnations as Krishna and Rama. The third eye can be viewed as the center of creation and imagination.

The third eye is symbolized as a transparent lotus flower with two white petals representing the ida and pingala (mystical spiritual channels) or Shiva and Shakti on the left and right, respectively. They are sometimes considered to be the unmanifest and manifest minds or the pineal and pituitary glands.

I've had a number of experiences with visualizing that may have had a connection to the third eye chakra. At one point as a young teenager I attended a poorly funded public school in Prattville, Alabama. The school had only one bus, which resulted in a long wait of an hour or more in the gym every day before classes would begin. In addition, the cafeteria could only hold about twenty percent of the student body at a time, resulting in another long wait sitting on the bleachers in the gym while everyone in the school took turns eating before the afternoon classes would begin.

During those hours of daily waiting, I read lots of books. When I got tired of that, I convinced a friend to play a game based on an experiment I had read about. In the experiment, a researcher created a set of five cards with different geometric shapes: a star, a circle, a triangle, a square and a diamond. One participant would look at the shapes and try to mentally send the image to someone else.

We decided to try the game ourselves. I created a set of the cards. She would look at a card and send me the image mentally. I discovered that if I closed my eyes, relaxed for a few seconds, and then opened them again, the symbol would appear on the wall across the gym. There was no guessing and no struggle. The image simply appeared.

When I tried to send the images to her, the success rate was very low. Perhaps I was a good receiver but not a good sender. Or maybe she was a great sender and anyone could have received the images she sent. No one else tried the game with us so we will never know.

Years later I tried another experiment. I was pregnant with my daughter and was taking breaks from work regularly to get a snack. I've never been patient with all the time that it takes to eat enough food to keep body and soul together. Now I was eating for two.

Someone suggested I use the time for visualization. I started imagining a beautiful yellow-pink rose. It was one of those roses that blends from yellow to peach and then to pink at the edges of the petals. I would hold that image in my mind while I ate several times a day.

Soon afterwards, I received a gift of a dress with pink and yellow roses and then a similar pair of pajamas. When my daughter was born, she had beautiful red hair and a gorgeous peach complexion, courtesy of her Norwegian heritage on my husband's side. Then, of course, we named her Rosemarie. That experiment yielded plenty of beautiful roses.

Around the time I started chanting, I also took an online meditation course that recommended focusing on the third eye. While taking the course and practicing daily, I started having an increasrd level of unusual experiences. This was low-level stuff in my own life, yet notable all the same.

For example, one night I woke up just after midnight and had the distinct feeling that I should leave my bedroom and go to sleep on my office floor. I was not excited about the prospect. My office does not have a bed. It is also in the basement, complete with the potential for spiders crawling on the floor. Nevertheless, I could not shake the feeling and could not go back to sleep. I gathered up my covers and pillow and headed for my office.

Within minutes of lying down on the floor, the phone rang. I jumped up and grabbed the phone. Someone was calling from India with services for my business. They had clearly neglected to take the time zone difference into consideration. I informed the caller that it was the middle of the night and I was not interested in talking business. The significance of the event was that my entire family could have been woken up by the phone if I had not been lying on the floor in my office when the phone rang. After I hung up, I went back to my bedroom.

Although I did not "see" anything associated with this or other similar experiences during the time that I was taking the meditation course and focusing on my third eye, this was a type of knowing that felt connected to the third eye rather than the kind of gut level knowing associated with the solar plexus. I had a clear sense of something to do or some place that I had to be.

My conclusion was that activation of the third eye could have immediate practical benefits, but I also felt strongly that I wanted to keep my chanting as a heart-centered practice rather than try to develop other spiritual abilities. I'd like to keep the development of the heart as my priority and trust that other spiritual gifts, such as the activation of the third eye, may grow naturally out of that focus.

That being said, the science of the brain and associated glands is fascinating. The connection between the pineal gland and altered states of consciousness has been well-established in the traditions of yoga and meditation, but little scientific investigation has focused on this tiny gland. Long revered by mystics, the pineal gland has often been considered a useless, vestigial organ by medical doctors. Yet the "eye of God" features prominently in many esoteric traditions and even appears on the American dollar bill. The pineal gland has occasionally been a focus of study in modern times, usually to determine a possible role in mental illness and psychotic states.

12 | Holding a Vision: Third Eye Chakra

One researcher, Rick Strassman, MD, spent five years conducting experiments with DMT, an endogenous, or naturally occurring, substance in the human body that causes psychedelic experiences when administered in large enough does. DMT is reputed to be released in the body (some suggest by the pineal gland) at birth, death and during times of extraordinary or life-threatening stress. Strassman devotes a couple of chapters in his book *DMT: The Spirit Molecule* to theories and research related to the pineal gland.

If the pineal gland is the seat of consciousness, the fact that there is a very large statue topped by the pinecone-shaped pineal gland in the Vatican is also fascinating. Did the early Catholics know the mystical teachings about the pineal gland? If so, how had the knowledge been lost? The name pineal comes from the Latin pinea or pinus, meaning pine cone. Representations of the pineal gland are used symbolically in art of the Sumerians, Egyptians, Indonesians, Greeks, Romans and Babylonians.

Some believe that we enter and leave our physical bodies at birth and death through the pineal gland. Other sources say that there is a whirring sound heard by the individual when the pineal gland is activated. This is represented in myth as a toy used by the god Bacchus as a child. A pinecone-shaped piece of wood wrapped with a cord gave out a humming sound as he spun the toy.

In most people, the degeneration of the pineal gland begins at the age of six or seven and continues until puberty. The interior of the pineal body contains follicles surrounded by connective tissue. The follicles consist of epithelial cells and calcareous deposits. In some reptiles the pineal gland serves as a light receptor. This connection may account for the serpent extended symbolically out of the forehead in the headdress of many Egyptian statues.

Another magnificent example of the pineal gland in art and architecture is the ancient temple of Angkor Wat in Cambodia. This temple graced the civilization of the Angkor people from about 800 AD until the fifth century. Angkor Wat literally means the "City of the Temple." The political hierarchy included a god-king surrounded by priests and high dignitaries. The civilization was based on agriculture and an irrigation system that controlled the water of the Mekong River.

Deities and Chants for the Third Eye Chakra

Krishna, one of the deities most closely associated with the third eye chakra, is the son of Devaki and her consort Vasudeva, king of the Chandravanshi clan. Devaki's brother was Kansa, an evil tyrant. He was told that a child of Devaki would kill him, so he set out to murder the young Krishna.

For his own protection, Krishna was sent to live in the country with Nanda and his wife Yasoda. Krishna's childhood was spent

Gopala

among their cow herds. This is the origin of Krishna's childhood names, Gopala and Govinda. "Go" means "cow," a sacred animal that may also symbolically represent sacred scriptures. "Go" is sometimes translated as "light."

The following is a chant to Krishna as Gopala:

> Devakinandana Gopala, Devakinandana Gopala
> Devakinandana Gopala, Devakinandana Gopala

This simple chant means that Gopala is the joy or bliss ("ananda") of his mother Devaki.

CHAPTER 13
Finding Unity: Crown Chakra

The seventh chakra is the crown chakra, the seat of enlightenment, known in Sanskrit as the Sahasrara chakra. Sahasrara means "thousand-petaled." According to Eastern traditions, the crown chakra is related to god-consciousness (samadhi) and the transforming powers of the divine. On the physical level, the crown is related to the nervous system and

Sahasrara Chakra

the brain. There is also a connection to the pineal and pituitary glands (similar to the third eye) and to the hypothalamus.

I recently heard a recording of a lecture by John Byde on politics, health and the history of consciousness.[11] He mentioned that the practice of wearing a gold crown would help to direct energy into the pineal gland and therefore help rulers to make appropriate decisions on behalf of their people. I had never thought about the purpose of a crown, or even thought that there was a purpose beyond some kind of fancy, expensive hat.

Crowns have traditionally been made of metals with a high degree of conducting power such as gold and silver. These metals are reputed to amplify the reception abilities of the pineal gland. Adding a variety of gemstones to the crown helps to fine-tune this process further. Byde actually made himself a metal crown with various stones that he said he wears under his hat in the winter. He says he does not wear it in the summer in public.

Even without the physical décor, we call the top of our heads the crown. A baby being born is "crowning" as their head reaches the end of the birth canal. Just below the crown are our temples. Byde discusses the architecture of physical temples and says that the traditional alcoves are a means of conducting the energy of the earth for enhanced spirituality and serve as a kind of wave guide. Perhaps the temples on the sides of our heads have a similar function.

The crown chakra is represented by twenty layers of fifty petals each. This chakra is sometimes thought to be a combination of a cluster of chakras on the skull, such as the back of the head where monks may gather their hair or shave a bare spot. The crown can be viewed as the father, or spirit energy, drawing the mother, or earth energy, from the lower chakras upward.

The dominating color of the crown chakra is white or gold. Reaching the crown chakra is largely equated with freedom from limitations and the boundaries of time and space. In this way, the crown is a link to the universal. Those who have advanced practice in meditation may feel that the confines of their minds and bodies have been swept away.

Perhaps this sense of unity with all of life experienced in the crown chakra includes a sense of merging with other people as well as the more generalized sense of merging with all of cosmos. I have had several spontaneous experiences of connecting to others that went beyond what I might view as normal empathy. I don't know if this is associated with the crown chakra at all. However, this kind of thing may be some small taste of the unity with all of life that others describe as part of crown chakra activation.

For me this experience has taken the form of sudden empathy or bonding with someone else. For example, one day several years ago I was shopping in Staples and turned to go down an aisle. I looked up and saw a man at the other end of the aisle with a large purple birthmark covering most of one side of his face. There was an instant connection. I felt energy passing through both of my hands like a healing response reaching out to him. Suddenly I had an uncanny sense of his whole life, including the challenges of his childhood growing up with such a significant discoloration on his face.

I was a little shaken. Neither of us said a word and he turned to leave the store. I went home and started cooking dinner for my family. In the process of making dessert, I was frying some homemade donut holes. One of them exploded and splattered oil on the right side of my face, the same side as the stranger's birthmark. The burn was not nearly as large as his birthmark, but it was the worst burn I've ever had and took weeks to heal. The coincidence was uncanny.

Most of us are conscious of the boundaries of our physical bodies ongoing. We can think about our hearts and feel them beating in our bodies. Or we can think about our toes or about our necks or our stomachs and know where they are located. In this way our attention is traveling within our physical bodies.

Perhaps if we start to recognize that our consciousness extends beyond our bodies into the whole universe, sometimes referred to as the body of God, then our consciousness becomes free to travel into any part of the universe or other dimensions and to connect with any part of life. Ultimately, this may even include what we view as non-sentient life.

If we share a single consciousness with all that exists, then it is not really a question of whether a mountain is sentient or a flower or a planet or a star has conscious awareness. Perhaps by extending our consciousness through the crown chakra, we can "ensoul" any part of creation. In that way we are one with everything. This might help us to live life completely and fully because there would be no fear of loss. If we are part of a unified whole, forms may change but the sum total is the same.

Deities and Chants for the Crown Chakra

One of the presiding deities for the crown chakra is Shiva—often depicted in a dancing form known as Nataraja—Lord of the Dance. Shiva is one of the principle deities of Hinduism, part of the trinity composed of Brahma, Vishnu and Shiva.

Shiva is the destroyer of evil, akin to the Holy Spirit in the Christian trinity. Shiva is alternately depicted both as benevolent and fearsome.

Shiva is often shown with a serpent around his neck, a crescent moon as an adornment, the river Ganges flowing from his hair or flowing nearby, the trishula as his weapon, and a damaru (drum) nearby. The dancing form of Shiva called Nataraja is a joyful being spinning and dancing through creation.

The following is a chant associated with Nataraja:

> Nataraja Dhimi Dhimi Bolo
> Nataraja Bam Bam Bolo
> Nataraja Sundara, Nataraja Shivaraja Sundara

"Dhimi dhimi" is the sound of Nataraja's dancing feet. "Bam bam" is his beating drum. "Sundara" means "beautiful" and "lovely."

13 | Finding Unity: Crown Chakra

Nataraja

Part III
Enhancing the Power of Mantras

Chapter 14
Synergy of the Body and Soul

I woke up in the middle of the night nearly a decade ago, overwhelmed and angry. I felt like I had been thrown into the game of life without a rule book. I had studied metaphysics and self-transformative practices for years, but my results at the time were sporadic. Sometimes life was wonderful. Sometimes I felt confounded with too many difficult challenges.

Then from somewhere the thought came to me: "I will put my laws in their inward parts, and in their hearts I will write them." This Biblical quote (Jeremiah 31:33) was only vaguely familiar to me. All the same, in that instant I knew that every bone and muscle and fiber of my being was the living, breathing rule book demonstrating the laws of life.

Everything I needed to know was literally written in every cell, organ and limb of my physical body. All I had to do was read the pulsating messages written in blood and sweat and flesh. My physical body was reflecting my thoughts and experiences. As others have said before me, biography had become biology. The invisible had become visible. I could read the script of my life–past, present and the trajectory for my future–in my physical form.

I believe that our bodies are designed to last in health and vibrancy for a long time, possibly for centuries, of creative, joyful living. The words and sounds that we choose to vocalize and those that we sing are creating and recreating us constantly. This is one of the reasons that I generally prefer chanting as a spiritual practice when compared with meditation or silent prayer. Sound affects matter. And that matters to me.

Unfortunately, our thoughts, feelings, beliefs, words and lifestyle choices are sometimes the weapons of our own chosen self-destruction. If we accept the premise that God, as the energy of life, is literally with us in every breath and heartbeat, we need only read the messages written in our bodies with true honesty and courage to know how to heal ourselves. This does not discount medical attention but is an adjunct to reasonable health measures.

This is not to judge ourselves or others for maladies of the body or soul, but a way to have compassion for ourselves and others. I will also say that there are saints among us that accept disabilities or diseases on behalf of others. Not everyone is the cause or source of their own suffering. Some conditions may be sacrificial and do not reflect the thoughts or consciousness of the person bearing that burden in any way.

Beyond Physical Health through Chanting

Ultimately my personal goal is to go beyond achieving physical health through chanting and other spiritual practices and move towards having a true synergy of the body and the soul. In many traditions the body represents the Divine Mother and the spirit is symbolized by the Divine Father. I would like to experience the spirit flowing through my body freely rather than feeling the need for unending control and discipline.

Even in intensive sports, there must be a way to channel energy so that the physical body does not break down from overuse. Why should the physical body deteriorate if it is a reflection and expression of the eternal spirit? This does not make sense to me. There are yogis and saints who display all kinds of supernatural abilities such as slowing or stopping their hearts or going into breathless states for extended periods of time. Why is this the exception and not the norm?

Maybe our bodies begin to fail because we are trying to strengthen and master the physical body through sheer force —manipulating muscles, bones and joints–rather than viewing the body as the pliable vessel of energy or spirit. Many martial arts masters do not necessarily even look strong, but they can do things that the strongest men in the world cannot do because they have learned to use their body as a channel for energy. There must be a way of channeling chi or prana so that the body is restored rather than destroyed in the process of living.

There have been miracle workers throughout the ages: Jesus and Buddha and Christian saints and Babaji and more. Babaji, an Eastern master and spiritual teacher, is called the Eternal Youth. He is purported to have lived for thousands of years, coming in and out of his body as desired or needed to assist mankind.

This is the stuff of legends to be sure, but science is also beginning to document individuals who can live without eating and those who are immune to poisonous snakes and those who live with little to no sleep. Stan Lee's episodic series called *Superhumans* documents many of these modern people with remarkable abilities.

Uniting the Body and Soul through Chanting

Chanting is a practice that unites the body and soul. Sound is a conduit between the world of the spirit or energy and the world of the earth. There seems to be a fairly direct conversion of energy into matter. Quantum physics is demonstrating that particles and waves merge and shift into one another constantly.

The work of Hans Jenny in the science of cymatics (see Chapter 16: Mantras and Yantras, pp. 105-116) demonstrates that forms are created by various tones and sounds. There is a clear congruency between sound and geometric forms. This directly ties into the practice of both mantras and the use of yantras or sacred geometry.

Creating a Celestial Body

When we speak, and especially when we chant or sing, we may be creating geometric forms in our own bodies and in the matter around us. This is quite a science and a lifetime study. There is also a concept in Christianity that one day we will have an eternal body: "this corruptible must put on incorruption" [1 Corinthians 15: 53]. This is called the "body glorious" or the "body celestial." The same concept exists in many religions in different forms: the idea that there is an eternal body that we can create or receive.

Chanting, toning and sacred singing are among the tools that have an impact on both matter and spirit. Perhaps a combination of efforts will lead to achieving an eternal form, if that is indeed desirable for one or many. Various other yogic techniques may also be part of the equation.

Chanting is a form of self-investigation. What feelings arise and what is the impact on the physical body? When you chant do you feel spacey or grounded or uncomfortable or elated? These may be keys to evaluating your own psychological and emotional states. I am fortunate in that regard: when I am chanting, I often feel like I am falling in love.

There seems to be a huge leap from the desire to simply be free of ailments of the body and mind to the possibility of an eternal body. I am fascinated by the research being done by scientists like Candace Pert who demonstrates how thoughts are converted to chemicals in the body.[12] There is also much work being done with somatic psychology, and even reports of people with multiple personalities whose physical forms change when they shift from one personality to another. There are records of people whose eye color, scars, eyesight and conditions like diabetes appear and disappear when they are existing as one personality versus another.[13] That is amazing.

All of these things show that the body is quite fluid. Perhaps the body is far more fluid than we have thought in the past. And anything that is fluid is instantly affected by sound. Sound is a bridge that unites the physical and the spiritual. That is a great place to start. A practice like chanting that involves the emotions, the mind, the heart and the physical body may allow ordinary, flawed people like me to transform ourselves into more glorious beings on one level or another. At least it is a grand experiment.

Ultimately a dedicated spiritual path, including whatever practices appeal deeply to you, can lead to a harmonious relationship between the body and soul. Maybe there are multiple answers to the long-standing question of old age, disease, and death. I am looking for a way to find those answers and to achieve results without going into a cave for a lifetime or more. For me, chanting is a path that can work on many levels while I am living in the modern world and fulfilling my responsibilities. There are other tools I have found to be helpful like breath-centered meditation and hiking in the mountains. However, chanting is my primary spiritual and self-creative practice.

CHAPTER 15
Sound, Color and Kirtan

Spiritual traditions worldwide view sound as the activating force in the universe. Sound is referred to as the Word, a fundamental energy or infinite vibration permeating all of cosmos. This can be actual words or the vocalizing of pure tones, sounds produced with or without a specific meaning attached.

Sacred Toning

Many sound healers use sacred toning to bring healing energy into the physical realm to serve as a vehicle for releasing imbalanced energy from the physical body or a particular environment. Toning often utilizes extended vowels in an improvisational fashion without adherence to a specific rhythm or melody. Sometimes this is similar to keening or wailing in grief. Other times it is simply a beautiful song of joy without words. Many indigenous peoples use forms of toning in rituals and ceremonies. When utilized as a spiritual practice, sacred toning is the use of extended vowels for the elevation of consciousness.

Healing with Instruments and Voice

Sound healing can also be done with musical instruments, tuning forks, Tibetan bowls or natural or man-made objects.

My own primary interest is in sound healing utilizing the voice. This is the origin of the term vocal medicine: using the voice through chanting, sacred toning and singing for healing and enlightenment.

The power of the voice is one of the most incredible tools available to all of us for self-transformation. For an individual, chanting, singing and toning are a type of self-created internal massage with sound. In a group, many voices blended together can create powerful harmonies that reinforce patterns of healing and rejuvenation.

The Creative Power of Sound

There are legends and stories in many traditions related to the miraculous power of a spoken command. In Christianity we find many references to this power in the Bible. The Genesis story is an account of creation through the spoken word. Other biblical passages reinforce this idea: "Thou shalt decree a thing and it shall be established unto thee" [Job 22:28, KJV].

There are also ancient Jewish legends about a golem or creature created from clay or mud. The golem is animated by inscribing a holy word in its forehead, accompanied by incantations using holy scripture. The power to animate matter with a spoken fiat has long been viewed as a truly godlike ability. The words chant, enchanted and incantation are closely related.

Among native peoples, chanting in unison for rain or for the recovery of someone who is ill are common practices. This type of shamanistic practice as a whole is experiencing a comeback in the modern world. We seem to know instinctively that sound is creative and affects the environment around us as well as our own bodies.

Combining Color and Sound

The human desire for invigorating combinations of sound and color is viewed by some anthropologists as a deep and ancient need. The brightly colored clothing of many native cultures worn during whirling dances seen against the flickering flames of bonfires likely had an effect similar to flashing strobe lights in modern animated films or discos. The merging of drumming, music, chanting and dancing with the visual stimulation of changing lights and colors can yield potent results.

Combining music with visualizations, sacred geometry or colored light creates a sensory immersion that can take the science of mantras and chanting to a whole new level. From the days of the ancient Greeks into contemporary times, mystics and followers of occult traditions have insisted that particular colors and certain types of music and rhythms possess the ability to induce trances and hypnotic states. Synchronized combinations of music and color may be even more powerful.

Sound and Color in Ancient Healing Temples

My own introduction to ideas related to sound and color healing came when I was a teenager. I attended a conference on the ancient healing temples of Egypt held at the Association for Research and Enlightenment in Virginia Beach, Virginia. The A.R.E. was founded to promote and preserve the work of Edgar Cayce (1877-1945).

Edgar Cayce, known as The Sleeping Prophet, was an American mystic who gave trance readings, usually to provide key insight for difficult medical cases. According to Edgar Cayce's readings, healers in the temples in ancient Egypt used combinations of color and sound not only to heal patients but also to reverse their age. During a reading, Edgar Cayce recounted a past life in which this was accomplished for him.

Cayce reported that he had been a priest in ancient Egypt and had gone out as a missionary preaching a relatively new, monotheistic religion. He returned to Egypt as a very elderly man over one hundred years old. He was taken into a temple and treated with sound and color therapy. This returned him to the health and biological age of a man in his twenties.

That story inspired my own lifelong passion for the use of sound, music, art and color for healing and transformation. Several events in my life in the last few years, including the use of visualization and guided meditations in the recovery of one of my sons from a traumatic brain injury (see end of this chapter), have reignited my desire to understand and further explore the healing power of the arts.

Using Multimedia Productions for Healing

One of my first experiences with the healing potential inherent in combinations of sound and color occurred just after high school when I was living with my grandparents in Los Alamos, New Mexico. I saw a flyer for an unusual healing therapy utilizing film. I decided to give the experience a try.

Upon arriving, I was asked to lay down under a pyramid structure with a lattice composed of crystals. After about twenty minutes I was taken to a room that was completely dark. I sat down in a comfortable chair in a reclining position, staring at the ceiling above me.

As soon as I was settled, a film began to play on the ceiling. The film consisted of sequences of colors and images of gemstones and crystals spinning and twisting in space. The music was relaxing and fairly nondescript. Overall the experience was pleasant and appealing. I did not have a strong reaction of any kind, but I was intrigued enough to convince a friend to come and try the experience herself.

She went through the same sequence of relaxing under the pyramid structure and then watching the film as I had done. For whatever reason, the experience for her was quite emotional. Something about the film touched her deeply. She was sobbing when the film ended. The practitioner checked with me to make sure that I would look out for her while she processed the experience through the remainder of the day.

I am not sure why, but we obviously had very different reactions. Although I had not noticed any significant impacts myself, she was clearly affected. That early experience impressed me with the idea that we are all unique in our responses. The experience also gave me increased respect for the potential therapeutic impact of multimedia productions.

The Art of Visual Music

One of the most promising and fascinating applications of multimedia therapy is a genre of abstract films that have been used for psychotherapy as well as pain reduction. This art form is called Lumia or Visual Music. These films are sequences of geometric forms, semi-realistic forms, or flowing colors combined with music. Women in childbirth have reported reduced levels of pain while watching this type of film. Other films have also been used to comfort veterans suffering from PTSD.

A specific series of these films by Cecil Stokes (known as the Auroratone films) included a sound track of organ music and singing. The sound of the human voice (Bing Crosby in a few of the films) was combined with instrumental music and abstract images to create films that were used to help WWII veterans to connect with their emotions and thus become more open to traditional psychotherapy. Many of these veterans were suffering from both physical and emotional wounds and were in need of deep healing.

Healing with Visual Music and Kirtan

I can envision applications of Visual Music in kirtan. Images and abstract color forms in films could be synchronized with chants. The idea is to create a multi-sensory experience that is specifically for therapeutic purposes, either for relaxation or the creation of elevated states of consciousness.

This would not take the place of more traditional kirtan, but could be designed like a multimedia sound bath with therapeutic purposes in mind. This is an area that I would like to understand more deeply in order to create the best possible experience of comfort and healing for participants.

In addition, some futurists believe that we will spend increasing amounts of time indoors in the coming decades and that problems with sensory deprivation and perceptual isolation may result. The use of art forms that affect multiple senses and participatory experiences like chanting and kirtan could help to combat this deficiency.

The Pokeman Shock Syndrome

In contrast with therapeutic applications, sometimes combinations of color and sound can actually cause harm. This is a further reminder of the power of multimedia arts. For example, recent studies of epilepsy have demonstrated that certain color and sound patterns in video games and animated cartoons can trigger seizures. The phenomenon known as Pokemon Shock is a dramatic example of this danger:

> On December 16, 1997, an episode of the then-unstoppable Pokemon animated series was broadcast in Japan. Barely thirty minutes later, nearly *700* children were on their way to hospitals.
>
> The episode, called "Electric Soldier Porygon," is now part of Pokemon folklore.... What caused all the problems were the animation techniques employed in the episode. There comes a point, around twenty minutes into the show, when Pikachu uses his lightning attack to blow up some missiles.
>
> ...[T]he animators used a rapidly-strobing technique that flashed red and blue lights on the screen... to make the explosion look "virtual"....
>
> And then all hell broke loose.
>
> Straight away, children across Japan were struck down with various ailments. Some kids passed out, or experienced blurred vision. Others felt dizzy, or nauseous. In extreme cases, some even experienced seizures and cases of temporary blindness.
>
> While the exact number of children legitimately affected by the show will likely never be known, in total 685 kids (375 girls, 310 boys) were put in

ambulances suffering some kind of medical problem after watching the episode.

While most made speedy recoveries—some within minutes...—a small number were diagnosed with epilepsy, which had been triggered by the rapidly-blinking display.[14]

In the aftermath of this disaster, the Pokemon show was taken off the air for four months. When it returned, the first episode back included an infomercial of sorts to explain what had happened and the precautions being taken going forward. The "Electric Soldier Porygon" episode was never shown again.

The Power of Repetition and Variation in Chanting

In contrast with the Pokemon Shock catastrophe, the human brain is soothed by the multisensory stimulation and the small irregularities that occur constantly in nature. A perfect example is the movement of leaves in trees combined with the sound of the wind. This is an overall experience with set parameters and small variations happening within those parameters. The leaves on a tree move sporadically with the wind, but always within the bounds of the reach of the branches and the stems of each individual leaf.

There is a great deal of this interplay between variation and regularity in chanting. A phrase or passage is repeated many times. There are variations that naturally occur in the human voice and in instrumentation with every repetition. A chant can be sung thousands of times and never be exactly the same. These are the types of slight irregularities the human brain craves.

Mantras have also traditionally been combined with yantras or images of deities as visual focuses (see Chapter 16: Mantras and Yantras, pp. 105-116). These experiences or practices may help to offset the detrimental effects of separation from nature itself or help to combat the pressures of detrimental forms of over-stimulation in modern times.

In addition, research in the field of neuroscience into cross-sensory connections indicates that vision and hearing are not nearly as separate as we might think. As early as 1927, the Russian investigator P.P. Lazarev determined that the sensitivity of the rods in the eye increased during acoustical stimulation. Another Russian researcher, P.A. Yakovlev, found in 1935 that "stimulation of the ear by sound conspicuously enlarged the area of the field of cone vision."[15] Sound and color seem to work together to enhance one another.

Chanting as Healing Prayer

Several years ago, one of my sons was in an accident on a mountain bike that resulted in a severe blow to his head. During his recovery over a period of about eighteen months, I walked him through visualizations almost every night to help him relax and sleep. The accident and its aftermath resulted in significant PTSD, which recurred again a few years later. I had begun chanting intensely by that time and added chanting to my practices for his healing.

Through that experience, I learned that chanting is not only for self-transformation. It can be a form of service for those around us as well. Chanting can be a means of sending positive energy to family and friends or into world situations or for the planet as a whole.

Chanting is a form of universal prayer that can be a blessing for those with specific needs or a general release of peace and healing. Although mantras and kirtan are most closely associated with Hindu and Buddhist traditions, chanting is a ubiquitous human practice. The desire to combine sound with color or other arts such as dance or film for potentially even more powerful effects also seems to be a cross-cultural phenomenon.

CHAPTER 16
Mantras and Yantras

There are ancient visual tools for meditation known as yantras that can be combined with mantras to accompany chanting and meditation. Yantras are geometric forms similar to mandalas that have been in use for thousands of years. Yantras can represent a specific deity or an aspect of God or a single sound. Yantras are mystical diagrams associated with particular thoughts and rituals.

The word "yantra" means "instrument." Yantras usually have a central form with shapes radiating out from the center, including triangles, circles, hexagrams, pentagrams, octagons, lotus petals and tridents. Each shape has symbolic importance. Any color utilized is also chosen for its inherent meaning.

There have been stones found in India with drawings of yantras dating back 10,000-12,000 years. The central point of a mandala or yantra is called the bindu. This is the same term that is used to refer to the dot applied to the forehead that represents the third eye. The yantra is a focus for visualization, one of the fundamental powers of consciousness.

Yantras are generally simpler and less colorful than the mandalas often associated with Buddhism. Yantras can sometimes be three-dimensional. Entire buildings (temples, cathedrals) have been constructed as yantras. In ancient India, building a temple and positioning a temple within a village was the most significant part of aligning the inhabitants' lives with the divine. The temple was built first. Residential dwellings and buildings for businesses and government facilities were constructed afterwards.

Private yantras may have been derived from the larger forms used in temple construction. As depictions of universal vibrations, yantras are a type of microcosm. Rituals involving mantras and yantras can become very complex. The rituals may be performed only on certain days of the year. The mantras are repeated with mathematical precision for each aspect of the yantra. The rituals are done at certain times of the day, and certain types of food or offerings are given.

Using Yantras with Mantras

Yantras can be invested with energy and activated by the use of mantras. The combination of mantra and yantra creates an energy field for a specific purpose. Yantras are a form of sacred geometry. Mantras are formulas of sacred sound. This creates a very powerful combination.

Yantras are sometimes used in vastu (the Hindu form of feng shui) to correct negative configurations or influences in the environment. Yantras are also worn as talismans or charms. Yantras can be created for specific purposes such as the mitigation of astrological influences, the healing of a particular disease, or for spiritual protection. Yantras may be guarded by Hindu priests to prevent unauthorized access to them.

Yantras tend to be linear and geometric, whereas mandalas are more figurative. Mandalas are often made from fragile or perishable materials or destroyed after creation to emphasize the impermanence of the world. The creation process itself is a meditation. On the other hand, yantras are retained as a channel and receptacle for divine energy.

Tantra, Yantra and Mantra

There are three basic forms of practice in Hinduism that are used individually or together for self-liberation. They are the path of action or physical practice (tantra, physical power, nervous system, nadis), the path of the mind and knowledge (mantra, thought power, invocation, devotion) and the path of will power (yantra, spiritual power, individual will, renunciation).

Each of these three practices can be used or misused. The key is the intention and purity of the practitioner. For example, in the worst-case scenario, mantras can be used to cause harm or create suffering (tamasic). They can also be used purely for self-centered reasons (sattvic). Ideally, they are used for universal spiritual liberation (rajasic).

Energizing a Yantra

Personally, I do not have a highly structured way to use yantras. I simply feel happy looking at these beautiful symbolic forms. However, if you are a person who derives comfort from ritual, you may want to consider the following practices in association with energizing a yantra:

- take a shower or bath to start with a sense of purity on the physical level
- find a place where you will not be disturbed (you may want to face east)
- light incense or diffuse essential oils (sandalwood, cedarwood, myrrh)
- create some kind of altar with special objects and/or fresh flowers
- state your intention or desire (either personal or universal)
- choose a set number of times to repeat the mantra (108 is a common number)

The Science of Cymatics

The science of cymatics relates directly to the art of yantras. Cymatics is a branch of research that explores the power of sound to change matter and to create stunningly beautiful or discordant patterns in sand, water and other materials.

The term cymatics was coined by Hans Jenny (1904-1972), a Swiss researcher who explored the nodal patterns formed by materials subjected to continuous sound. The patterns for specific sounds such as "om" are remarkably like the forms depicted in traditional yantras. The Sri Yantra, for example, is the visual equivalent of the sound Om.

The following pages contain some of the more common yantras, their meanings and associated mantras. Each yantra has a specific use and potential spiritual power.

The Sri Yantra

The Sri Yantra is a 12,000-year-old symbol known as the holy wheel. The Sri Yantra represents the union of the divine masculine and feminine. This is symbolized by nine interlaced triangles with upward triangles meeting downward triangles in

Sri Yantra

a kind of star tetrahedron. There are forty-three intersecting triangles organized in nine concentric levels radiating out from the central bindu point.

The outer square represents the earth element and forms a stable and solid foundation for the yantra. The square is the power of condensation and manifestation into the world. The four doorways or gates are the thresholds into the outer world. The circle in the center brings focus to the visual form and the mind of the viewer.

The lotus petals represent creation and life force. Some teachings view the Sri Yantra as a map of man's spiritual journey from the outer to the inner along designated circuits. The following is the mantra associated with the Sri Yantra. This is a mantra dedicated to Lakshmi and is also known as the Maha Lakshmi Mantra or the highest mantra to the goddess Lakshmi. Thus, it is sometimes viewed as a wealth mantra.

> Om Shrim Hrim Shrim
> Kamale Kamalalaye
> Prasida Prasida
> Shrim Hrim Shrim
> Om Mahalakshmayai Namaha

As noted in Chapter 5: Sounds of the Cosmos (pp. 33-40), the bija syllable shrim helps to attract people and situations that are beneficial. Hrim energizes the heart. This mantra helps to manifest vitality and abundance in all of life.

Hrim and shrim are often used together. Hrim is solar, shrim is lunar. "Namaha" means "it is not about me" or "not me." Kamale is a reference to the purity of the lotus flower. Kamalalaye relates Lakshmi to this purity and expands on the beauty of the lotus. Prasida is a request for blessings from the Divine Mother. "Mahalakshmi Namaha" means "to give honor and surrender to the greatest or highest form of Lakshmi."

The name Lakshmi is derived from the Sanskrit root "laks," to perceive or know, and is related to "lakshana," meaning "target" or "aim." This suggests that abundance is achieved through perceiving and aiming for your chosen target.

The Sri Yantra and the Maha Lakshmi Mantra reinforce both divine reality and the receiving of material prosperity. This allows for leadership that is inspired and beneficial for all.

The Ganesha Yantra

The Ganesha Yantra utilizes many of the same basic shapes as the Sri Yantra. The six-pointed star is a simplified version of the nine interlocking triangles of the Sri Yantra. The mantra associated with this symbol is "Om Gam Ganapataye Namaha" and means "Salutations to the remover of obstacles!"

Ganesha is the master of both inner and outer journeys. Ganesha is known for knowledge, patience, preparation and grounding. The sheer weight of an elephant is a wonderful metaphor for the earth-based energy necessary for successful

Ganesha Yantra

projects and endeavors. The energy of Ganesha can form a strong foundation for a new business, for example. Ganesha can help to clear away uncertainty and self-doubt.

The six-pointed star symbolizes balance and harmony. Ganesha is the patron of the arts, crafts and sculpture. When colored, the Ganesha Yantra usually includes deep, rich earth colors like forest green, golden yellow, primary red and orange.

The Surya Yantra

The mantra associated with the Surya Yantra is "Om Hram Hrim Hraum Sah Suryay Namaha." As the god of the sun, Surya brings illumination, healing and spiritual magnetism. The yantra

Surya Yantra

and the mantra are both tools for guiding the thoughts and feelings in healthy patterns, but the viewer's intention is paramount.

The Surya Yantra is sometimes called the Radiance Yantra. The twelve outer petals are known as the celestial beams of the sun. They are symbolic of the twelve months of the year and the twelve astrological signs. The sun is the regal master of the entire solar system and the visible universe.

Focusing on the Surya Yantra can be particularly appropriate for extending yourself into new social situations, travel or undertaking adventures in life. Surya is a celebration of light and illumination in yourself and others. When colored, the Surya Yantra is decorated with flaming red, orange, silver and gold.

The Hanuman Yantra

The mantra associated with the Hanuman yantra is: Om Hanumate Namah. The combination of Hanuman's mantra and yantra helps to center the heart to overcome difficult situations. Hanuman is often appealed to for solutions in seemingly impossible circumstances.

Hanuman Yantra

Hanuman is known for fierce loyalty and unfailing energy. Hanuman's yantra is a good choice for focusing on supporting your immune system, increasing your productivity and helping with effective communication skills. Some sources say Hanuman protects against malefic influences from a challenging placement of Saturn in your astrological chart. Other sources say the same thing about an ill-placed Mars.

The Hanuman Yantra is associated with strength of mind as well as body. This is the kind of strength needed to confront and triumph over the hurdles in life. Hanuman encourages straightforward communication and clear thinking.

The Durga Yantra

The mantra associated with the Durga Yantra is "Om Aim Hrim Klim Chamundaye Viche." The word "Chamundaye" is a reference to Durga and the slayer of Chamunda, an evil demon.

Durga Yantra

"Viche" means a "shield" and indicates Durga's role in protecting her own. Durga has the role of destruction for the sake of universal harmony. The Durga Yantra and mantra are based on the consciousness that it is better to proactively divert misfortune whenever possible.

For this reason, the Durga Yantra is viewed as a protection yantra. Durga is a warrioress with indomitable strength. Like Kali, she will help you to let go of anything that is no longer serving you. In addition, she can serve as a shield on many levels as you move through the world.

Durga cultivates a unique combination of fearlessness, courage and love. The many upward pointing triangles in the yantra emphasize spiritual freedom. Durga's colors are white, silver, gold, saffron, orange and red.

The Gayatri Yantra

Gayatri is a Vedic poetic meter of twenty-four syllables or any hymn composed in this meter. Hence, there exists a whole family of Gayatri Mantras, all of which serve as meditative aids. The yantra is the visual counterpart for this family of mantras. The most well-known of the Gayatri Mantras is the following:

> Om bhur bhuvah svaha
> Tat savitur vareñyam
> Bhargo devasya dhīmahi
> Dhiyo yonah prachodayat

The first line is actually an invocation and is not technically part of the original sacred text from which the mantra is drawn. The meaning of this mantra can be broken down word for word:

Om: the primeval sound
Bhur: the physical body and physical realm
Bhuvah: the life force or mental realm
Suvah: the soul or spiritual realm
Tat: God as That, like the Hebrew I AM That I AM
Savitur: the Sun, Creator or Source of all life
Vareñyam: adore
Bhargo: effulgence of divine light

Devasya: the supreme
Dhīmahi: to meditate
Dhiyo: the intellect
Yo: may this light
Nah: our
Prachodayāt: illumine or inspire

The general meaning would be something like this: "Let me meditate on the most adored Lord and Creator, whose divine light illumines all realms (physical, mental and spiritual). May this divine light illuminate my life!"

Gayatri Yantra

A more extended meaning would be: "O God, the Protector, the basis of all life, Who is self-existent, Who is free from all pains and Whose contact frees the soul from all troubles, Who pervades the Universe and sustains all, the Creator and Energizer of the whole Universe, the Giver of happiness, the most Excellent, Who is Pure and the Purifier of all, let us embrace that very God, so that He may direct our mental faculties in the right direction."[16]

Part IV
Songs of Transformation

Chapter 17
Finding Bliss through Kirtan

Kirtan is a platform for a profound sharing of energy, heart, and soul. A case could be made for the idea that this is the deepest possible level of intimacy. After all, the heart and soul are the deepest places in our beings, and a chant is a tangible release from those places.

The chants that are being sung in kirtan are vibrating in every cell and at every level of the being of each person participating. That sound joins with sound that has been vibrating in every cell of the bodies and in the hearts of everyone else present. The sounds merge together completely, passing through everyone equally and synchronizing breath and heartbeat.

Kirtan is the most profound sense of actually embodying God in a physical way that I have yet encountered. Filling oneself with sacred sound creates a oneness with life and energy and source that can be profoundly moving. The experience of merging with something more powerful than yourself and with the others in the group can create something personal and spiritual and tribal, all at the same time.

How well you sing or whether you are a trained singer is not a pertinent issue. No prior musical experience is required. Kirtan is ideal if you are self-conscious about singing because your voice will blend with everyone around you. Best of all, science has shown that group singing changes the chemistry of the brain and the body. These changes happen irrespective of skill level. Clearly you do not have to have professional experience as a singer to reap the benefits of chanting and kirtan.

Kirtan and the Brain

Group singing brings the individual into harmony with the group as well as the sound itself. There are physiological processes at the root of the sense of connectedness and social flow. Oxytocin and dopamine (feel good chemicals) are both released, and cortisol (a stress chemical) is reduced. Oxcytocin means "quick birth," a reference to the first bonding experience in life between a mother and her infant. Oxytocin also has a broader role in mediating social and emotional behaviors.[17]

Interestingly, sometimes professional musical performance can have a negative impact on body chemistry, increasing levels of cortisol. Singing in a group generally reduces levels of cortisol. The sense of elation in group singing may come from endorphins, a hormone released by singing, which is associated with feelings of pleasure.[18] Group singing has been studied as a successful antidote for depression, stress and isolation.

The Process of Kirtan

A concept related to the benefits of group singing is referred to as flow. Improvisational music in particular creates a feeling of flow, which is akin to being "in the groove" or being lost in the music. Chanting shares this concept with jazz music as well as with other genres such as gospel and blues. There is also a social aspect to flow as musicians and singers coordinate with each other.

The kirtan leader begins a chant and usually determines the length and pace of the chant, which can vary from a few minutes to an extended period of time. Sometimes it is a drummer who determines the pace of the chant and has the role of keeping in touch with the level of engagement among participants. Typically a chant will start slowly, speed up with the repetition of a line or verse, and then slow down again at the conclusion. Alternately, the pace of the chant may be unchanged but the volume of the music may become softer to indicate the end of the chant.

The pace can also vary back and forth within a chant. In addition, the same phrases may be repeated with a new melody. Instrumentalists may play solos for a while and then group chanting resumes. This creates a high level of interdependence among the musicians and the participants and further fosters the sense of being in the moment, similar to the concentration that happens during meditation. Studies indicate that improvised musical experiences elicit higher levels of social flow and bonding than highly regulated music.

The Format of Kirtan

Chanting has been practiced in a call and response format in many spiritual traditions. This is sometimes hierarchical: a priest or guru chants a line and the congregation or devotees respond. This is not always the case in kirtan in the Western world, which can be done as call and response or in a sing-along style. However, lines are generally repeated twice in either format, making the chants easy to learn.

I tend to emphasize simple, singable chants in the kirtans that I lead. I don't want either the words or the melodies to get in the way of participation for anyone who wants to chant. In fact, I've even set kirtan lyrics to nursery rhymes for kirtans specifically designed for families and children. I also lead a significant number of chants in sing-a-long style, especially if many of the participants are new to kirtan. That way no one has to worry about singing at the wrong time.

The Instruments of Kirtan

Kirtan is often accompanied by a harmonium. The first time I heard chanting accompanied by a harmonium, I knew immediately that I had found something very special. The harmonium is a small keyboard instrument with a hand-pumped bellow and two sets of internal reed pipes for treble and bass notes. The level for each is controlled by metal stops on the front of the instrument. Sound is produced when a key is pressed, allowing air to flow over the reeds.

The harmonium sounds something like a cross between a small organ and a bagpipe. I love the eerie, longing tone. The sound is continuous, either a stable or melodic drone, depending on the playing style. This is perfectly suited for both Eastern chants and some Western hymns. In addition, the harmonium is an acoustic instrument, easy to play in a variety of circumstances.

The drone of the harmonium establishes a tone that sets a foundation. Some musicians view this as a masculine energy that forms a backdrop against which the feminine energy of creation plays with melody, rhythm and improvisation, moving from dissonance to harmony and back again. This generates a unique sound. Just hearing the sound of a harmonium creates a relaxation response for me.

Chants also lend themselves to accompaniment by other instruments such as hand drums or cymbals (kartals) or tabla. The tabla is an Indian drum that takes many years of practice to learn. Playing tabla is quite complex rhythmically and tonally. All kinds of other acoustic and electronic instruments are being used as part of kirtan: guitars, cellos, violins, flutes and more.

The Role of Harmony in Kirtan

Another aspect of music is the concept of harmony. Harmony is the use of multiple tones within a structure such as a chord. Barbershop and choral singing are both examples of vocal harmony. Harmony is typically a Western approach to group singing. Harmony is also possible with Hindu, Buddhist, Sikh or other chants. However, harmony may not always be desirable in kirtan when viewed as a musical meditation.

Some proponents of kirtan and chanting advocate singing only in unison. Paramhansa Yogananda, one of the early Indian teachers to introduce chanting to Americans, explains this perspective in his book *Autobiography of a Yogi*. He states that in Indian music the melody (the relation of successive notes) is stressed, rather than harmony (the relationship between different simultaneous notes). Yoganada believed that singing in unison supported an emphasis on the individual's communion with God through a simple and direct expression of praise rather than the potentially more horizontal focus on harmonizing with other voices. Yogananada describes his view of the purpose of kirtan in the following passage:

> The *sankirtans* or musical gatherings are an effective form of yoga or spiritual discipline, necessitating deep concentration, intense absorption in the seed thought and sound. Because man himself is an expression of the Creative Word, sound has the most potent and immediate effect on him, offering a way to remembrance of his divine origin.[19]

Personally, I have experienced positive benefits with both approaches. When everyone sings exactly the same melody, there are less distractions and a certain unified power that is created. On the other hand, having some participants sing in harmony creates a fuller sound with its own beauty. Although I do not try to teach or lead harmony in kirtan, anyone who has the skills, independence and confidence to harmonize with the chants is always welcome to add their own unique interpretation.

Kirtan Repertoires

Kirtan repertoires may be specific to a particular tradition, such as the chants associated with kundalini yoga or the Vedic mantra tradition. Kirtan events may also include chants from a wide variety of traditions. I tend to sing mostly from the Hindu tradition, with a few Buddhist and Christian chants for variety. I generally also make it a practice to sing at least one chant in English in the course of an hour or two of kirtan music. The familiarity of English can be a great comfort for Western participants.

Whatever the tradition or focus, chanting is a joyful way to concentrate the mind, eventually allowing the singer to go beyond the mind. This is aided by the repetitive nature of the words. The fact that many chants are in Sanskrit can be a good thing rather than a hindrance in this regard. I prefer to use very simple Sanskrit phrases rather than complex Vedic poetry or texts. I find for myself that when I am less focused on the pronunciation and the meaning of the lyrics, more time can be spent on simply participating in the sound and in the feeling of bliss.

Variations in Kirtan

One of the wonderful things about kirtan is the ever-changing nature of this art form. The same simple chant is never exactly the same. There is a principle in the visual arts of "regular irregularity." The human eye and ear are designed to notice and pick up small variations in the environment like leaves rustling in the breeze. Those small variations keep life and art and music interesting while staying within given parameters for comfort and stability.

The Multidimensional Nature of Kirtan

The vast majority of the time, kirtan stays comfortably within powerful and what I would deem to be normal parameters. Occasionally I have also had a clear sense of the fact that sound indeed reaches across dimensions. Once when leading kirtan in an open-house kind of situation, people were coming and going continuously. There was only a small group present at any given time. I had my eyes closed much of the time while chanting. I had the repeated experience of thinking that a large number of people must have come into the room. I kept hearing what sounded like a full choir chanting, but every time I opened my eyes, there was only a handful of people in front of me.

Another time I heard a flute-like instrument playing along with the chant I was leading. I assumed that my husband, a member of my kirtan band, was playing his recorder. He often goes back and forth between playing an Udu drum and his recorder. Every time I looked over, I was surprised to see that he was playing his drum. Afterwards I mentioned this to another band member who said, "What? He wasn't playing his recorder tonight? I kept hearing that, too!"

I don't know what these kind of experiences mean or if they mean anything at all. As I mentioned, they are rare. I've lead kirtan for well over a hundred events of various types in the last few years and those two incidents are the only times I've heard anything really unusual. I am not trying to create any kind of phenomena at kirtan. The joy of sharing sacred music is enough. I mention them only because they are reminders for me that there are mysteries and potentially deeper levels within all forms of art and spiritual practice.

A different kind of multidimensional experience occurred at another point when I was traveling and staying at the home of a friend. A family member had died fairly recently. Other family members were still mourning their loss. I felt such intense grief there that I hardly slept the first two nights. Fortunately I had chanting as a tool. I chanted alone those first few days in the hours when I couldn't sleep, and I also attended kirtan one evening. I was hopeful that chanting and kirtan might help to alleviate the situation in some way.

There was a sense of connecting to a tangible but unseen dimension. By the third night something seemed to have shifted or cleared. I could finally sleep and the visit was ultimately a positive experience.

Spiritual Protection and Kirtan

The concept of spiritual protection afforded by guides, angels, devas or other benevolent beings is a key principle in nearly every religious tradition. These beings guard the devotee during spiritual practices and ongoing in life. I do not think a discussion of any spiritual practice would be complete without mention of the potential need for spiritual protection.

In Christianity, angels are supernatural beings who often serve as messengers or intermediaries between God and humanity. The theological study of angels is vast. Angels may serve as personal protectors (guardian angels) or as powerful beings who battle evil and defeat devils and demons. Many depictions of Archangel Michael, for example, show him wearing military-style armor, brandishing a sword and standing on the head of the devil.

This is remarkably similar to the roles of the Hindu goddesses Kali and Durga, who are known as fierce warriors. Both are depicted with many arms and many weapons to defeat the most recalcitrant demons. The idea of personal guardian angels is also present in Hinduism. Some sources view these guardian angels as a combination of two different spiritual concepts. These concepts are the devas and the atman as explained in the following passages:

> Devas are deities who help guard people, pray for people, and promote the spiritual growth of people and other living beings like animals and plants....
>
> The atman is a divine spark inside each person that acts as a higher self to direct people toward higher levels of consciousness.[20]

Based on your own traditions and beliefs, you may want to surround yourself with angels or other guardian beings or simply with white light as part of your practice of mantras, chanting and kirtan.

Kirtan and Community

One of the great joys of kirtan is the sense of community combined with chanting as a spiritual practice or sound meditation. As Mike Cohen states in his booklet *Bhakti & Beyond*, "The practice of kirtan is experiential, not conceptual." In addition, the practice is shared:

Kirtan is communal. It helps us connect deeply with others by coming together and creating a powerful, Divinely musical experience together …. And this communal experience is primal!

In Kirtan you don't show up as an audience member who listens to a group of professional musicians. You show up as a participant, a member of a tribe, who is guided into and helps create a powerful musical/spiritual experience.[20]

Chanting can create positive relationships with others during the shared experience of kirtan. I have found deep connections and friendships through this practice. And I have learned to let go. Music cannot be held the way that a child or a painting can be held. Every chant is different, every time. You have to be in the present. You have to be in the moment. You have to let go of the past to sing a new song. Perhaps that is the deepest transformation of all.

CHAPTER 18
Goddess Chants

As far back as ancient memory reaches, the Great Mother has been honored around the globe. There are goddesses from virtually every culture and time period: Hindu, Christian, Egyptian, Celtic, Norse, Aztec, Mayan, Babylonian, Greek, Roman, African, Buddhist and more. Over the past couple of millennia, most cultures gradually lost their traditions surrounding the Divine Mother. However, in the last decade or two there has been a resurgence of interest in goddess spirituality.

Goddesses are the protectors of mantra, creativity, self-realization and self-transformation. Some goddesses are gentle and loving, others are wrathful and menacing. Goddesses generally bring spirituality down to earth in the sense of assisting us in materializing desired outcomes.

Within the Christian tradition, the original Hebrew pantheon also included many goddesses. The worship of female deities was later suppressed. It is believed that Shekinah, the consort of Yahweh, was removed from the Old Testament around 400-500 BC. Another goddess in the original Hebrew tradition was Asherah, the wife of El, described as "she who walks in or on the sea." The chants in this chapter are from Hindu, Buddhist and Christian traditions.

Chant to Mataji

Mataji is the sister of Babaji, the eternal youth. She is purported to appear sporadically to devotees and pilgrims, able to manifest in either a spiritual or physical form.

"Adi" means the "primal" or first mother. "Jai" means "victory." The basic meaning of this chant is "Victory and honor to the Divine Mother Mataji!"

Mataji requested of Babaji that he always retain a physical form that would be visible to at least a small number of disciples. Babaji granted his sister's request. To this day, they are both sought after by devotees hoping to catch a glimpse of their physical forms.

The story of Babaji and Mataji came into prominence as described in Paramhansa Yogananada's book *Autobiography of a Yogi*. Babaji appeared directly to Yogananada as well as to others, including Lahiri Mahasaya and Sri Yukteswar Giri.

Mataji

Yogananada writes that Babaji appeared to him before he left India to go to America, assuring him that his mission was in keeping with Babaji's desires to spread Kriya Yoga in the West.

Adi Mataji
Adi Mataji, Adi Mataji, Namo, Namah
Mataji Mama, Mataji Mama, Mataji Mama
Mataji Mama, Mataji Mama
Jaya Ma, Jaya Ma, Mataji Mama

Chant to Saraswati

Saraswati is the Hindu goddess of music, art, speech and wisdom and the consort of Brahma, one of the three deities in the Hindu trinity. For more information about the seed syllable "aim," see Chapter 5: Sounds of the Cosmos (pp. 33-40).

Aim Saraswati
Om Aim Saraswati Namaha
Om Aim Saraswati Namaha
Aim, Aim, Aim, Aim
Mahadevi Saraswati Namaha

Bhajamana Ma!

Bhajamana Ma! is a directive to the mind to meditate on the Divine Mother. The melody includes several abrupt rests and is a play on the idea that the mind begins to wander and is brought to a sudden stop and returned to focus. There are fifty names of the Divine Mother in this chant. The chant contains the following names of the Divine Mother, infinite in her variations and facets:

Ananda Mayi Ma: the mother overflowing with bliss
Durga: protective mother of the universe
Lakshmi: goddess of wealth, fortune and prosperity
Saraswati: goddess of wisdom, music and the arts
Jugadambe: mother of the world
Parashakti: mother of cosmic energy
Adi: the first or primal mother
Kali: goddess with mastery over time and death
Sita: goddess of good character and happiness
Tridevi: goddess of the trinity (Hindu Trimurti)
Brahmani: she who is the power of Brahma
Kriyashakti: she who manifests all things
Chandi: she who is ferocious against evil
Maha: great or the great mother
Shivapriya: the beloved of Shiva
Mahadevi: she who is the soul of the universe
Pranashakti: she who is the breath of the universe
Mata: mother, a term of honor
Radha: beloved of Krishna
Ama: mother goddess
Parvati: goddess of love and devotion
Malini: fragrant mother
Vedamata: mother of the Vedas (sacred texts)
Kundalini: mother of the primal energy of the spine
Nitya: the eternal mother
Ajha: the unborn or birthless mother
Adishakti: mother of the primal or first energy

Shivapara: she who is the supreme consort of Shiva
Mahesvari: Durga, reference to the Mahesvar river
Satya: mother of truth
Devi: the divine feminine or goddess
Gauri: Parvati, she who has a white complexion
Bilvani: mother of the woods
Kevada: mother of the kevada flower
Mahamaya: Durga, the cause of creation
Ganga: mother of the Ganges river
Lola: mother of movement, mother of sorrows
Mahakali: the great Kali
Yogeshwari: Durga, she who fulfills desires
Mahavidya: the great mother of knowledge
Medha: the intelligent mother
Dipta: Lakshmi, the shining mother
Sati: mother of mindfulness and awareness
Sarada: mother of the harvest
Bhagini: honorary title for sister, Lord Indra's sister
Yogamata: mother of yoga

Bhajamana Ma!

Ananda Mayi Ma, Bhajamana Ma! (2x)

Verse 1: Jai Durga Lakshmi Saraswati Jugadambe Parashakti Adi Jai Kali Sita Tridevi Brahmani Kriyashakti Ma!
Verse 2: Jai Nitya Ajha Adishakti Shivapara Maheshvari Satya Jai Devi Gauri Bilvani Kevada Mahamaya Ma!

Jai Kudalini Ma, Jai Kundalini Ma (2x)

Verse 3: Jai Chandi Maha Shivapriya Mahadevi Pranashakti Mata Jai Radha Ama Parvati Malini Vedamata Ma!
Verse 4: Jai Ganga Lola Mahakali Yogeshwari Mahavidya Medha Jai Dipta Sati Sarada Bhagini Yogamata Ma!

Bhajamana Ma, Bhajamana Ma! (2x)

Bhajamana Ma!

Kathleen Karlsen

Chant to Kali

Kali is the goddess who defeats all, including death. Her name comes from the Sanskrit root meaning "time." Although fearsome, she is the most loving of all mothers because she liberates her children by removing all illusions. Those who do not fear the dissolution of their lesser attachments see her as overflowing with love.

Jai Ma Kali
Jai Ma Kali Namo
Jai Ma Durge Namo
Kali Ma, Durge Ma
Jai Ma Kali Namo
Kali Ma, Durge Ma
Jai Ma Durge Namo

Chant to Lakshmi

This mantra means "Goddess Lakshmi, reside in me and bestow thy abundance on all aspects of my existence." The name Lakshmi is derived from the Sanskrit root "laks," to perceive or know, and is also related to "laksana," meaning "target" or "aim."

As noted in Chapter 4: Formulas for Freedom (pp. 21-32), Lakshmi is the Hindu goddess of wealth and prosperity. Lakshmi is usually depicted with gold coins flowing from her hands.

In Hindu mythology, Lakshmi was born from the churning of the primeval ocean. Lakshmi is the consort of Vishnu, one of three persons in the Hindu trinity. With Parvati and Saraswati, she herself is part of the Tridevi, or a holy trinity of goddesses.

The seed syllable "hrim" is the sound of divine power. Shrim (or srim) is related to growth and development. See Chapter 5: Sounds of the Cosmos (pp. 33-40) for more details.

Lakshmi Bhayo Namaha
Om Hrim Shrim Lakshmi Bhayo Namaha

Om Tare Tuttare

This is the Green Tara Mantra which means "I bow before Tara, the Mother of the Victorious Ones." "Tare," "Tuttare" and "Ture" are variations of Tara's name. This chant is said to liberate from suffering, fear and disease.

In the Tibetan pantheon of deities, Tara is the consort of the Dhyani Buddha Amogasiddhi. Her name means "star." Tara also exists as a goddess in many traditions and countries, including Hinduism, Polynesian mythology, Druidism, Finland (Tar, Woman of Wisdom), Roman mythology (Terra, Earth Mother), and South America (the goddess Tarahumara).

Om Tare Tuttare
Om Tare Tuttare Ture Svaha

Chant to Pandaravasini

This is a chant to Pandaravasini, the consort of Amitabha. Her name means "the White Robed One" which suggests that she is vested with purity.

Pam is her seed syllable. She holds her hands together at her breast in the anjali mudra. This is the prayer mudra with hands together in front of the heart, often used to open and close yoga practices.

Her mantra is "Om Padmadevi Pushpadevi Pam Svaha." "Padma" means "a lotus flower" and "devi" means a "goddess" or "queen." "Pushpa" also means "flower." The mantra honors Pandaravasini as the goddess of lotuses and queen of flowers.

Pandaravasini is one of the five female Buddhas associated with the five male Dhyani Buddhas. The five Dhyani Buddhas are said to have existed since the beginning of time. They represent or symbolize divine principles or forces. They are self-born.

The Dhyani Buddhas are not historical figures like Gautama Buddha. The word dhyani is derived from the Sanskrit dhyana meaning "meditation." The Dhyani Buddhas are also called Jinas, meaning "Victors" or "Conquerors."

The five Dhyani Buddhas and their divine consorts are:

- Vairochana and Akasha-Dhatvishvari
- Akshobhya and Lochana
- Ratnasambhava and Mamaki
- Amitabha and Pandaravasini
- Amoghasiddhi and the Green Tara

See the book *Female Deities in Buddhism: A Concise Guide* by Vessantra for additional details. A full reference is included in the Bibliography (see p. 168).

Padmadevi Chant
Om Padmadevi Pushpadevi Pam Svaha

Chapter 19
Chants for Peace

The search for peace on this planet seems to be ubiquitous throughout all ages and cultures. Chanting, meditation, and breathing are all fantastic for calming anxiety and agitation and helping to nurture inner peace. Peace is generally defined as a lack of conflict and as the presence of harmony. A legal definition of peace is a state of security, enforced by law or custom.

For decades I thought that if the right people banded together and worked for world peace, the world would be peaceful at last. I joined several different spiritual organizations. I met incredible people and had some amazing experiences. There are uncounted numbers of truly dedicated people working for peace, yet somehow peace is still fleeting at best.

Now I see establishing peace within myself as my primary goal. Peace is not necessarily lack of action, but a sense of unified action. When I feel sure that my chosen course is the best option for my life, then I feel peaceful in the midst of activity and outer pursuits.

Returning to the center of my being on a regular basis through chanting and other spiritual practices helps to maintain a sense of peace. The following chants are focused on peace at all levels.

Breathe Through Me

The Hebrew word for spirit is "ruach," which means "air in motion." This word also means "breath" and "life." When God speaks all of creation into being, it is His breath that carries the words that result in form.

Breath also refers to the cycle of breathing. The effects of controlled breathing can be remarkable. Shallow breathing, deep breathing, circular breathing (a technique used by musicians to create continuous tone for wind instruments), and rhythmic breathing can all be used to create different states of mind.

The word "prana" also means "energy, life or breath." Prana is the sea of energy that animates all life. This is the same as chi, qi or ki. All are descriptors of the fundamental energy of life, which in turn creates the building blocks of all matter and manifestation.

Breathe Through Me
Holy Spirit, breathe through me!
Holy Spirit, breathe through me!
Send your light through my soul:
Holy Spirit breathe through me.

19 | Chants For Peace

Hamsa Chant

The word "hamsa" means "swan." Hamsa is used as a device in meditation to focus on the inhalation (ham) and the exhalation (sa). Some authorities use the syllables in reverse: sa followed by ham.

The word "soham" can be used for the same purpose: "so" as the sound of inhalation and "ham" as the sound of exhalation. Soham can be translated as I Am He or I Am That. The use of "hamsa" or "soham" during chanting or meditation gives a focus for the mind.

Paramahamsa means "the highest swan" and is a term of respect for teachers regarded as having the highest level of attainment.

Hamsa Chant
Hamsa Hamsa (2x)
Hamsa Hamsa Hamsa (2x)

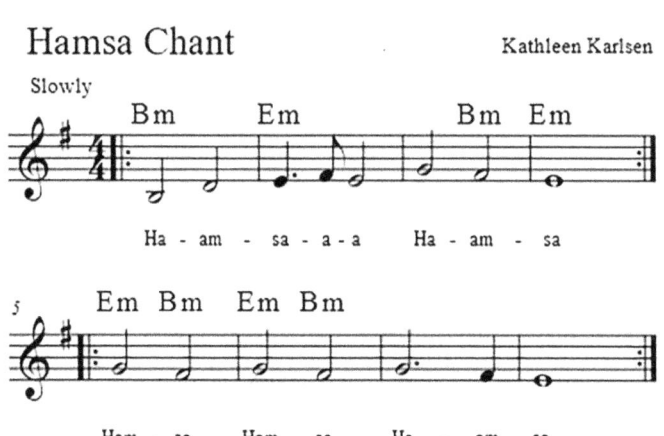

Chant to Lalita

The story of Lalita unfolds in the Brahmanda Purana, a thousand-year-old text in India. The name "Lalita" means "she who plays." Lalita is often associated with the color pink. She is both sensuous and motherly.

Background: the demon Bhanda had an extraordinary power. When he fought his enemies, half his opponent's power would be transferred directly to him. The sage Narada warned that only worship of Lalita could save the other gods from Bhanda's power. Narada was saying that it is the divine feminine personified by Lalita which gives every victory. That is how Bhanda was eventually defeated.

Lalita is highly independent. She insists on retaining complete freedom: "Whatever I say or do is according to my will alone. Whichever man accepts me as his must also accept my complete independence." Lalita is a consort of Shiva, signified by the garland she places around his neck.

Lalita exists in a perpetual state of perfect harmony, ever benevolent, her eyes moist with compassion for all beings. Lalita is portrayed as a young woman holding five arrows made of long-stemmed flowers (symbolizing love), a bow made of sugarcane, a noose, and a goad. The arrows are our five senses and the bow with which they are dispatched is our mind.

When we find ourselves pausing on the spiritual path, distracted by one thing or another, Lalita gently prods us along with her goad. If we resist her mild suggestion that it is time to move forward in our spiritual life, she lassos us with her noose and drags us, like misbehaving children, back to her lap.

Lalita has over a thousand names describing her many facets. Lalita's beauty is noted in the term "sundari" meaning "beautiful." "Ma amba" means "mother of the universe" and "shanti" means "peace." This chant can be translated as "Victory to Lalita, the beautiful goddess who is the Mother of the universe and brings peace."

19 | Chants For Peace

Lalita Shanti Om

Shanti Shanti Om, Shanti Shanti Om,
Jaya Ma Lalita Shanti Om
Ma Amba Jaya Ma Lalita, Devi Devi Sundari Jaya Ma, Shanti
Shanti Shanti Om, Jaya Ma Lalita Shanti Om

Lalita Shanti Om — Kathleen Karlsen

Lokah Samastah

This chant is a mantra of peace and blessings meaning: "May all beings be happy and free, and may my life contribute to the happiness and freedom of others." This chant is often used as a prayer at the end of a yoga session or meditation practice. It is an ancient mantra dating back centuries or millennia.

"Lokah" means "universe," "realm" or "location." "Samastah" is a reference to all living or sentient beings. "Sukha" means "happiness" or "joy." Sukhino is the happiness that comes from being free from suffering. Bhav is a state of union with the divine. "Antu" is similar to "amen," meaning "may it be so." Antu can also signify a vow or pledge.

This chant is a reminder that our actions and thoughts affect all of creation. It is something along the lines of the Golden Rule: Do unto others as you would have others do unto you. Variations of this sentiment are present in every spiritual tradition. This mantra invokes a state of compassion for all life.

Lokah Samastah
Lokah Samastah Sukhino Bhavantu

19 | Chants For Peace

The Three Jewels

This is a traditional chant which I found through a fairly circuitous route. One night I dreamt that I went out into my backyard and there was a small pond. (I do not actually have a pond in my backyard.) There were three ducks swimming on the pond. They were wild ducks, gray and brown in color.

One of the ducks dipped under the water, ostensibly to get some food. When the duck popped back up, he had transformed into a brilliant royal purple. The second duck went under the water. When it bobbed back up to the surface, he was a gorgeous sapphire blue. Finally the third duck went under the water and returned to the surface as an intense emerald green. Each time this happened, I was delighted and amazed.

The dream made such an impression on me that I started searching online for possible interpretations. In general, ducks symbolize good fortune. Because ducks can swim, walk or fly, they represent flexibility and the ability to adapt to changes. Birds are a connection between the physical world and the spiritual world. They symbolize spiritual freedom. The thought occurred to me that the ducks were like three beautiful jewels.

Searching on the concept of three jewels led me to this beautiful traditional Buddhist chant. Going for refuge to the Three Jewels (Triratna) is the unifying factor in all the varying forms of Buddhism. This ideal is also known as the three treasures, the cornerstone of living a spiritual life.

Translation:
   To the Buddha for refuge I go (the teacher)
   To the Dharma for refuge I go (the teachings)
   To the Sangha for refuge I go (the community)

The Three Jewels
Buddham Saranam Gacchami
Dhammam Saranam Gacchami
Sangham Saranam Gacchami

CHAPTER 20
Chants of Divine Love

Love is the power and bliss that is central to the practice of chanting or any form of devotion and union with the divine. Ultimately, I suppose all chants are chants of divine love. There is a feeling in great music and inspirational art that goes beyond words. I think this is a concrete form of love.

As human beings, the love between a mother and child is one of the deepest bonds that we experience, if we are fortunate enough to have parents who dedicate decades of their lives to our well-being. For me, the first few weeks after the birth of each of my children were an incredible sense of oneness. Some of my favorite memories are sleeping on my back with a newborn baby on my chest, completely at peace and completely in love with the little child entrusted to my care. In spite of increasing responsibilities as my family grew, I hardly wanted to sleep in those early weeks, not wanting to miss a moment of that sense of union. Ideally, that bond comes very close to the love between the soul and God.

The following chants exemplify several types of divine love: the love between a mother and son (Devakinandana Gopala), the love for the Creator (Gayatri Mantra), the love for a personal guru (Jai Issa Gurudev), the love of the divine personified as male and female consorts (Sita Ram), and the love of God in nature (May I Sing of Thee?).

Devakinandana Gopala Chant

"Devaki" means "shining one." Devaki is Gopala's (Krishna's) mother. This is a chant about the love between a mother and her son. I can relate. In addition to my daughter Rose (my oldest child), I have four sons.

More information about Gopala and Devaki can be found in Chapter 12: Holding a Vision: The Third Eye Chakra (pp. 80-81).

Devakinandana Gopala
Devakinandana Gopala
Devakinandana Gopala
Gopala Gopala
Gopala Gopala

20 | Chants of Divine Love • 151

Gayatri Mantra

This is an ancient mantra with a beautiful traditional melody. Gayatri is sometimes viewed as a personified form of the Vedas, or as the Mother of the Vedas. She is the consort of Shiva in his highest form as Sadashiva. See translation and meaning of the Gayatri Mantra in Chapter 16: Mantras and Yantras (pp. 114-116).

Gayatri Mantra
Om bhur bhuvah svaha
Tat savitur varenyam
Bhargo devasya dhimahi
Dhiyo yonah prachodayat

Jai Issa Gurudeva

There are many legends that Jesus spent the "lost" years of his life (ages 13-30) studying with Hindu sages. He is known in the East as Saint Issa. Others say that he spent time in Britain.

In 1887, a Russian war correspondent, Nicholas Notovich, claimed that he had been shown a document called "Life of Saint Issa, Best of the Sons of Men" while he was staying at the Hemis Monastery in Ladakh, India. This became a highly controversial claim, argued and publicly discredited by many scholars.

Others besides Nicholas Notovich, including Swami Abhedananda and the Russian painter Nicholas Roerich, also claimed to have seen manuscripts or heard tales of the studies and travels of Jesus in India. These stories have been debated hotly for over a century.

Other legends describe time that Jesus spent in Great Britain as a boy. These stories claim that Jesus traveled with his uncle, Joseph of Arimathea, to live in Glastonbury. This connects Jesus with the Arthurian legends and the Holy Grail. Some legends claim that Joseph of Arimathea served as a foster father for Jesus after his own father Joseph died. Some believe that Jesus studied the traditions of the Druids while in England.

The idea that Jesus would have traveled either to the East or to Britain to study is revolutionary. If Jesus himself studied multiple spiritual traditions, this widens the scope of religious "truth" significantly. Perhaps even more importantly, it may indicate that his spiritual path was progressive and required effort on his part.

This contradicts the idea that he was simply born as God Incarnate without the need to learn and perfect himself in any way. Personally, I find great comfort in the merging of East and West. Jesus was the guru of my childhood and has been an ongoing spiritual teacher in my adult life. This song brings together my love of Jesus with my love of mantras, chanting and kirtan.

Jai Issa Gurudeva

Hare Om, Issa Om, Gurudeva
Hare Om, Issa Om, Gurudeva
Gurudeva Issa Namah
Jai Issa Namaha Namo Namah
Jai Issa Namaha Om Issa Om

"Gurudeva" means "a spiritual teacher in masculine form." This chant means "Honor and victory to Issa, the highest teacher and expression of God!"

Chant to Sita and Ram

Sita refers to the Hindu goddess, Sita. Her consort is Ram or Rama. Sita is the main female character in the Hindu epic poem, the "Ramayana," and is an incarnation of Lakshmi, while Rama is the central male character and an incarnation of Vishnu. Sita and Ram are viewed as the ideal spouses.

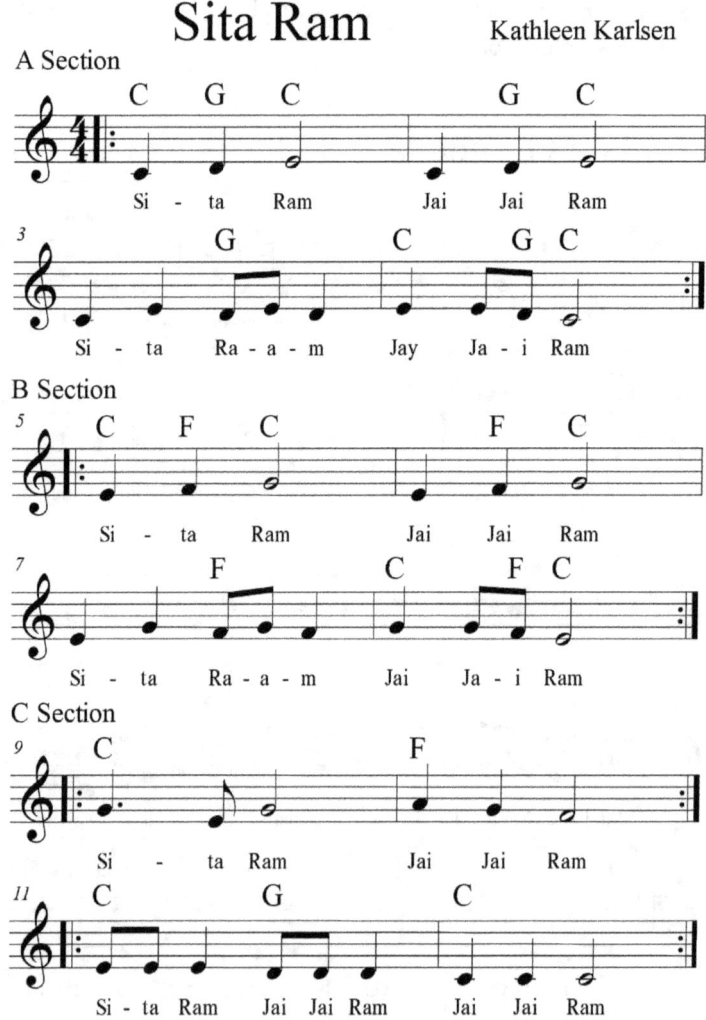

May I Sing of Thee?

I had someone express to me shortly after I began leading kirtan that I should only sing songs within my own cultural and religious heritage. In other words, I should only sing Hindu chants if I have a guru in a Hindu lineage. I should only sing Buddhist chants if I have the approval of a Buddhist monk and so forth.

My first reaction was that God belongs to all cultures and traditions. These traditions are my heritage as a soul. That being said, I also saw the wisdom and authenticity in chants acknowledging my own Celtic heritage: an approach to Christianity steeped in honoring God in all of nature.

I particularly love the idea of God in the stars and throughout the entire universe. In the Catholic tradition, Saint Patrick merged the love of God in nature inherent in the Irish people with his own love of Jesus and the biblical God. This chant is inspired by the poetry and prayers of Saint Patrick. Below is an excerpt from of one of the many variations of Saint Patrick's prayer for protection:

> I arise today, through
> The strength of heaven,
> The light of the sun,
> The radiance of the moon,
> The splendor of fire,
> The speed of lightning,
> The swiftness of wind,
> The depth of the sea,
> The stability of the earth,
> The firmness of rock.
> I summon today
> All these powers between me
> And those evils,
> Against every cruel and merciless power
> That may oppose my body and soul.

May I Sing of Thee?

May I sing of the glory of the stars?
May I sing of Thee?
May I sing the ancient harmonies?
May I sing of Thee?
May I know the brightness of the sun?
May I sing of Thee?
May I know the sweetness of your love?
May I sing of Thee?

May I Sing of Thee?

Kathleen Karlsen

Bb Drone; Guitar Capo: 3 (G)

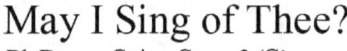

CHAPTER 21
Chants of Victory

The victory over our own vulnerabilities is the sweetest victory of all. The metaphor of the sun is an appropriate image in this regard. When the sun shines light on all of our own weaknesses, yet we still go forward to love to the best of our abilities, the reward for our labor is the peace of knowing that we have given our all.

One of the fun things about chants of victory is the opportunity to identify with the superheroes of the East: Ganesha, Hanuman, Nataraja and the many forms of Shiva. Our modern superheroes have their antecedents in the heroes of ancient mythology. It is exhilarating to connect with feats of superhuman strength, amazing abilities and valiant striving. Mythology is a highly relatable way to understand the human psyche and be inspired on the endless quest for embodied divinity.

We celebrate the best of human achievement in so many arenas: physical prowess, mental abilities, emotional stamina, endurance and loyalty. From the stories of the amazing feats of Hercules to the tall tales of Paul Bunyan in the early American wilderness, it is universally uplifting, inspiring, humorous and delightful to imagine the possibilities in life when normal limitations have been suspended. The following chants emphasize joy and overcoming.

Chant to the Sun

The sun is the original and possibly the ultimate representation of God as the giver of life. Sun worship is common in virtually every culture. Surya is the name of the sun god in Hinduism. More information about Surya and astrological chants can be found in Chapter 4: Formulas for Freedom (pp. 29-32).

Chant to the Sun
Om Bhaskaraya Vidmahe
Om Maha Tejaya Dimahe
Om Surya Namaha
Om Surya Om
Tanno Surya Prachodayat
Tanno Surya Prachodayat

21 | Chants of Victory

Chant to Ganesha

Ganesha is the Hindu god known as the overcomer of obstacles. Chants to Ganesha are often sung at the beginning of kirtan. The idea is to use the energy of Ganesha to overcome any obstacles to the kirtan itself. More information about Ganesha can be found in Chapter 16 : Mantras and Yantras (pp. 110-111) and Chapter 7: Establishing Safety: The Base Chakra (pp. 51-54).

Ganesha Sharanam
Ganesha Sharanam Sharanam Ganesha
Ganesha Sharanam Sharanam Ganesha
Sayesha Sharanam Sharanam Ganesha Sharanam
Sayesha Sharanam Sharanam Ganesha Sharanam

Chant to Nataraja

Nataraja is the dancing form of Lord Shiva. Dhimi dhimi is the sound of Natarja's dancing feet. Bam bam is the sound of his beating drum. "Bolo" means "I sing." This chant means: "I sing of Nataraja's dancing feet and beating drum."

Sundara is the masculine form of the Sanskrit term sundari meaning "beautiful." Nataraja is a beautiful, whirling form of Shiva. See Chapter 13: Finding Unity: The Crown Chakra (pp. 86-87)for more information on Nataraja.

Nataraja Sundara
Nataraja Dhimi Dhimi Bolo
Nataraja Bam Bam Bolo
Nataraja Sundara
Nataraja Shivaraja Sundara

Chant to Shiva

"Shambo" or "shambho" means "auspicious one." "Mahadeva" means "the highest God." "Shankara" means "the doer of good deeds." Shiva is the third god in the Hindu triumvirate, akin to the Holy Spirit in Christianity.

Shiva Shambo
Shiva Shambo, Shiva Shambo
Hare, Hare, Hare, Shiva Shambo
Om Shiva Om, Shiva Mahadeva Om
Om Shiva Om Shiva Om
Om Shiva Namah Shivaya
Om Shiva Namah Om

ENDNOTES

Chapter 1: Reforge Your Heart with Mantras

[1] Prophet, Mark and Elizabeth Clare Prophet. *The Science of the Spoken Word.* Summit University Press, 1983.

Chapter 2: The Science of Mantras

[2] Morelle, Rebecca, "Choir singers synchronize their heartbeats," BBC News, *Science and Environment*, July 9, 2013.

[3] National Research Council, *Learning, Remembering, Believing: Enhancing Human Performance.* Washington, DC: The National Academies Press, 1994.

[4] Susan Moran, "Mantras 101: The Science Behind Finding Your Mantra and How to Practice It," *Yoga Journal*, March 20, 2018.

[5] Marilyn Mitchell, M.D., "Dr. Herbert Benson's Relaxation Response: Learn to counteract the physiological effects of stress," *Psychology Today*, March 29, 2013.

[6] Hall, Manly P. *The Pineal Gland: The Eye of God, Man the Grand Symbol of the Mysteries*, p. 334. Los Angeles, CA: The Philosophers Press, 1937.

[7] Joel Blanchard, "How to Heal Your Pineal Gland to Facilitate Enlightenment and Optimize Melatonin and Live Longer," p. 5. Lexington, KY: 2013.

[8] Hartzell, James. "A Neuroscientist Explores the Sanskrit Effect," *Scientific American*, January 2, 2018.

Chapter 4: Formulas for Freedom

[9] Winerman, Lea. "A laughing matter," *Journal of the American Psychological Association,* June 2006, Vol 37, No. 6, p. 58.

[10] Myrtle Fillmore, "How I Found Health" (pamphlet), 1970, Unity Village, MO: Unity School of Christianity.

Chapter 13: Finding Unity: The Crown Chakra

[11] Byde, John. "Hacking the Pineal Gland," September 14-16, 2012: Eternal Knowledge at the Over the Moon Festival. https://youtu.be/MPwB7HlmJMs.

Chapter 14: Synergy of the Body and Soul

[12] Pert, Candace. *Molecules of Emotion.* New York, NY: Simon & Schuster, 1997.

[13] Goleman, Daniel. "Probing the Enigma of Multiple Personality," *The New York Times,* June 28, 1988, www.nytimes.com.

Chapter 15: Sound, Color and the Arts

[14] Plunkett, Luke. "The Banned Pokemon Episode That Gave Children Seizures," February 2011. https://kotaku.com/5757570/the-banned-pokemon-episode-that-gave-children-seizures.

[15] Allen, Frank and Manuel Schwartz. "The Effect of Stimulation of the Senses of Vision, Hearing, Taste and Smell Upon the Sensibility of the Organs of Vision," *The Journal of General Physiology,* 20 Sept. 1940, p. 105.

Chapter 16: Mantras and Yantras

[16] Ram, Sai, "What is the meaning of the Gayatri Mantra?" June 18, 2017, www.quora.com.

Chapter 17: Finding Bliss through Kirtan

[17] Keeler, Jason R., Edward A. Roth, Brittany L. Neuser, John M Spitsbergen, Daniel J. M. Waters, and John-Mary Vianney, "The neurochemistry and social flow of singing: bonding and oxytocin," *Frontiers in Human Neuroscience,* September 23, 2015, 9:518.

[18]Hom, Stacy, "Singing Changes Your Brain," *Time Magazine*, 2013, www.ideas.time.com/2013/08/16/singing-changesyourbrain.

[19]Paramhansa Yogananda, *Autobiography of a Yogi*, New York, NY: Philosophical Library, 1946, p. 159.

[20]Hopler, Whitney. "Guardian Angels in Hinduism," https://thoughtco.com/guardian-angels-in-hinduism. June 7, 2018.

[21]Cohen, Mike. *Bhakti & Beyond: A Bhakti Yoga Perspective on Kirtan*, Boulder, CO, 2008, p. 7.

BIBLIOGRAPHY

Ashley-Farrand, Thomas. *Shakti Mantras: Tapping into the Great Goddess Energy Within.* New York: Random House, 2003.

Cohen, Mike. *Bhakti & Beyond.* Boulder, CO, 2008.

Frawley, Dr. David. *Mantra Yoga and Primal Sound: Secrets of Seed (Bija) Mantras.* Twin Lakes, WI: Lotus Press, 2010.

Goodchild, Chloe. *Awakening Through Sound.* Boulder, CO: Sounds True, 2007.

Hartzell, James. "A Neuroscientist Explores the Sanskrit Effect," Scientific American, January 2, 2018.

Hay, Louise. *Heal Your Body: The Mental Causes for Physical Illness and the Metaphysical Way to Overcome Them.* Carlsbad, CA: Hay House, Inc.,1984.

Hom, Stacy. "Singing Changes Your Brain," Time Magazine, 2013.

Khanna, Madhu. *Yantra: The Tantric Symbol of Cosmic Unity.* London: Thames and Hudson Ltd, 1979.

Prophet, Mark and Elizabeth Clare. *The Science of the Spoken Word.* Summit University Press, 1983.

Ozanich, Steven Ray. *The Great Pain Deception.* Silver Cord Books, 2011.

Paramhansa Yogananda, *Autobiography of a Yogi*. New York: Philosophical Library, 1946.

Sarno, John E. M.D., *The Divided Mind*. New York: Harper-Collins, 2009.

Segal, Inna. *The Secret Language of Your Body*. New York: Simon & Schuster, Inc, 2010.

Shapiro, Deb. *Your Body Speaks Your Mind*. Boulder, CO: Sounds True, 2006.

Tomlinson, Sarah. *Coloring Yantras: 24 Sacred Symbols for Meditation, Healing, Abundance and Creativity*. Boulder, CO: Shamballa Publications, Inc, 2017.

Vessantra. *Female Deities in Buddhism: A Concise Guide*. Birmingham, UK: Windhorse Publications, 2003.

INDEX

A
Adrenals, 11
Ajna, 11, 75
Anahata, 63
Artha, 50
Ayurvedic, 24

B
Babaji, 93, 130-131
Bija, 33, 35-39, 109
Bladder, 17, 55
Brahma, 34, 35, 40, 51, 52, 86, 132, 133
Buddhism, 53, 61, 65, 105, 139, 147
Bagalamukhi, 36, 37

C
Chandi, 40, 133
Circle, 67, 109

D
Devaki, 80, 150
Dharma, 50, 147
Digestion, 60
Divine Mother, 5, 35, 92, 129, 133
DMT, 78-79
Dopamine, 120
Drone, 122
Durga, 39, 113-114, 125, 133-134

E
Ears, 68, 75
Endorphins, 120
Epilepsy, 98-99
Esophagus, 68
Eyes, 11, 26-27, 75, 94

F
Feet, 28, 49

G
Ganesha, 51, 53, 58, 110-111, 157, 159
Golem, 98
Gopala, 80-81, 150
Govinda, 80
Gut, 27-28, 59-64, 78

H
Ham, 18, 70, 143
Hanuman, 65-66, 112-113
Harmonium, 7, 121-122
Heart, 3-5, 9, 10, 17, 18, 35-39, 45, 61, 63-65, 109, 119, 139
Himavan, 58
Hips, 49
Hypothalamus, 11, 84

I
Ida, 76
Indra, 51, 134

J
Jainism, 35, 53, 61, 65
Jesus, 93, 138, 152, 155

K
Kali, 38, 40, 125, 133, 134, 136
Kama, 50
Kartikeya, 58
Kidneys, 17, 55
Kirtan, 7, 64, 101, 103, 119-127, 155, 159
Krishna, 38, 73, 76, 80-81, 133, 150
Kundalini, 38, 43-45, 50, 123, 133-134

L
Lam, 18, 55
Legs, 49
Liver, 17, 25, 38, 60
Lumia (visual music), 100
Lungs, 17, 36, 63

M
Manipura, 59-60
Mantra Purusha, 24
Mantra Yoga, 5, 9, 24
Marmas, 24
Meditation, 4, 10, 34, 37, 75, 77-78, 85, 105-106, 121-122, 126, 139, 141, 143, 146
Melatonin, 11
Meridians, 11
Moksha, 50
Muscular system, 49

N
Naad Yoga, 5
Nadis, 107
Nataraja, 86-87, 160
Neck, 68

O
Om, 6, 18, 22, 24, 33-35, 108, 114
Oxcytocin, 120

P
Pancreas, 17
Parvati, 36, 53, 57, 58, 76, 133, 134, 137
Pelvis, 43, 49
Pineal gland, 11, 12, 75, 78, 79, 84
Pingala, 76
Pituitary gland, 11, 75, 76, 84
Prajapati, 61
Prana, 34, 36-38, 62, 93, 142
PTSD, 100, 102

Q
Queen Mena, 58

R
Rajasic, 107
Ram, 18, 55, 154
Reproductive organs, 55

S
Sadashiva, 72
Sahasrara, 83

Sanskrit, 5, 12, 17, 22, 24, 33, 38, 49, 50, 60, 124
Saraswati, 35, 52, 58, 132-134, 137
Sattvic, 107
Shakti, 35, 36, 38, 40, 76
Shiva, 6, 34, 40, 53, 72-73, 76, 86, 160, 161
Skeletal system, 49
Solfeggio, 15
Spine, 34, 43, 44, 49, 133
Square, 50, 109
Stomach, 25, 27, 60
Surya, 30, 111, 112, 158
Svadhishthana, 55

T

Tamasic, 107
Tantra, 106, 107
Teeth, 11, 68
Thalamus, 11
Throat, 17, 18, 67-72
Thyroid, 11, 26, 68-72
Toning, 46, 94, 97
Triangle, 50, 64, 67, 107-110, 114

V

Vam, 18
Vastu, 106
Vedic astrology, 37
Vishnu, 34, 37, 57, 76, 86, 132, 137, 154
Vishuddha, 67
Visualization, 26, 46, 77, 98, 101, 102, 105

Y

Yam, 18, 55

ABOUT THE AUTHOR

Artist, author, musician, composer and entrepreneur, Kathleen Karlsen is the founder and owner of Living Arts Enterprises, LLC. Following her lifelong passion for sharing the transformative power of the creative arts, Kathleen has authored hundreds of articles and presentations; designed over seventy exhibits of her inspirational paintings; taught music and art to children and adults for more than a decade; and utilized her vocal talents as a professional narrator for educational videos.

Most recently, Kathleen has been composing her own unique kirtan music while sharing and exploring the sacred music of East and West. Her first album (Vocal Medicine with Kathleen Karlsen) is a companion to this book.

Kathleen has a bachelor's degree in studio art from the College of William and Mary and a Master of Arts in humanities from California State University. Kathleen lives in Bozeman, Montana. She and her husband Andrew have five children.

ABOUT THE ILLUSTRATOR

Rose Karlsen has studied drawing, film, photography, graphic design and set design. Her beautiful illustrations have graced magazine articles, advertisements, newsletters, postcards and a variety of business and marketing communications. Rose's illustrations are currently being utilized for the creation of a line of custom cards and gifts.

ALSO BY THIS AUTHOR

Flower Symbols: The Language of Love
Discover the Meaning of Flowers
in Folklore, Religion and Popular Culture

This book includes fascinating information about the symbolism and folklore of the world's most beloved flowers, with illustrations of selected flowers, famous quotes about flowers, selected poetry featuring flowers, and information about traditional uses of flowers for healing.

Flowers accompany us in nearly every major event in life: birth, graduation, marriage, holidays, illness and death. In addition, flower images adorn practically everything around us: hair, clothing, jewelry, wallpaper, furniture, artwork and more. Understanding the folklore, meaning, facts, stories and legends about the amazing world of flowers adds a new dimension to every aspect of life.

Reviews

"This little book reveals special meanings that different flowers have for humanity, and it has inspired in me a deeper appreciation for the unique blossoms of nature. While it seems we give flowers for gifts and to show we care all the time, this books gives further explanation as to what we might be communicating and sharing with others when we relate with flowers in art or on the doorstep." Alethea L., Home Educator

"This book shares detailed information with a joyous heart. Well researched and hard to find information included in each chapter. *Flower Symbols* is a great book to give as a gift." Maria L., Aromatherapist

Flower Symbols can be purchased at kathleenkarlsen.com.

ACKNOWLEDGEMENTS

My deepest gratitude to friends and family who have helped me with the creation of this book.

Thank you to my editor and dear friend Theresa McNicholas for your incredible attention to detail as well as your profound understanding of my intent and the purpose of this book.

Thank you to my daughter Rose for your beautiful illustrations. They have added immeasurably to the text. Thank you for your work on layout and book design. I am grateful for your talent and patience with my seemingly endless requests for more illustrations as the book progressed.

Thank you to Jake Fleming for assistance with the music: for teaching me how to use music transcription software at the start, and for contributing your expertise with chord choices and final tweaks to the musical notations in the end.

Thank you to Mahima Giri for her review of the first draft, especially the Sanskrit words and lyrics.

Thank you to my husband, Andrew, for your technical expertise, the wonderful cover design and your ongoing support in my life.

The Lord your God is with you,
the mighty warrior who saves.
He will take great delight in you;
in His love he will no longer rebuke you,
but will rejoice over you with singing.

Zephaniah 3:17, *Holy Bible,* New International Version

www.ingramcontent.com/pod-product-compliance
Lightning Source LLC
Chambersburg PA
CBHW050637300426
44112CB00012B/1841